You Are a
DIAMOND

You Are a
DIAMOND

Seeing Your Life Like a Diamond:

Volume I

Scratching the Surface

Yvan Kaprielian

YOU Are a DIAMOND
Seeing Your Life Like a Diamond: Volume I
Copyright © 2021 by Yvan Kaprielian

Although every precaution has been taken to verify the accuracy of the information contained herein, the author and publisher assume no responsibility for any errors or omissions. No liability is assumed for damages that may result from the use of information contained within.

Library of Congress Control Number: 2021923270
ISBN-13: Paperback: 978-1-64749-648-7
                ePub: 978-1-64749-649-4

Printed in the United States of America

GoToPublish LLC
1-888-337-1724
www.gotopublish.com
info@gotopublish.com

Dedication

To the People of the World
The chapters in this book could be worth your weight in gold,
If you open your heart and dare to be bold.
May they bring you brilliance
Whether it is now or later in your existence.
In the next pages of this manuscript,
The diamond mystery for you I will decrypt.
With a little openness of mind,
You will realize that you are the real diamond mine.
With willingness, practice, and meditation,
Helping you balance all facets of your well-being is my intention.
Your brilliance does come from within,
And you will find a way to show it, I imagine.
As you walk your path toward enlightenment,
The steps will be shown to you in increments.
Mighty is the power of the Light.
All aspects of your life can be like the Sun, golden and bright.
Blessings be with you and your family,
And may you find your happiness internally.
So be it!

Acknowledgements

To the Divine Light

To my beloved parents, my brother Stephan, and all my family members whom have contributed greatly to my growth.

To my beloved and respected spiritual teacher, Grand Master Choa Kok Sui, for the constant blessings, the teachings, and the guidance, especially for the ones that I do not yet have the capacity to understand and recognize.

To Dr. Glen Mendoza and Marilag Mendoza, senior disciples of GMCKS, for their friendship, mentorship, and support when I needed it the most.

To my friend and mentor Gerry Zoppi for countless hours of selfless support and guidance over the years.

To all my true friends and loved ones who have always stood by my side and ceaselessly believed in me.

Thank you to all.

Contents

Foreword

Spiritual practice is about finding a proper level of balance that best suits your life. I believe one facet of spiritual practice is sharing the Divine Light evenly in every aspect of your life. Character building, as Grand Master Choa Kok Sui teaches, is one of the main pillars to proper spiritual growth. Proper character building is initiated by balancing one's lifestyle, which is made up of diet, exercise, family, career, contribution through service and tithing, relaxation, finances, meditation, and so forth. Our external perception of the world is a direct reflection of our internal world. With this in mind, I will give you my personal life analogy... Diamonds!

You probably know that Diamonds are expensive. You probably also know that Diamonds are about light, reflection, dispersion, and brilliance. And you probably also know that Diamonds are very difficult to cut. Well, you're right! But do you know why they are so difficult to cut? Well, it's all about the facets.

First, the Master cutter has to map out the Diamond in the rough. Second, he has to start the process with an initial cut. The third step is the longest and the most difficult, but it is also the most important— faceting. As the Master fashions each facet, he makes sure that they are all symmetrical, well balanced, and in perfect harmony with one another. The Master understands that the better balanced the facets, the higher the brilliance. The Master constantly monitors the faceting process until it reaches a stage where dispersion of light is even. A diamond cannot have optimum brilliance if its facets are not properly balanced.

Every aspect of your life mirrors the facets of a diamond. They must be properly balanced. The interrelationship of each facet is critical in receiving the light and reflecting it back. The more balanced the facets of your life are, the easier it is to receive Light and to illuminate your world, both internally and externally. This will automatically and effortlessly give you the ability to create a very brilliant life.

By now you're probably wondering why I capitalized the word *Diamond.* Well, it's simple. Your life is the Diamond. What about the Master cutter? Who is he? He is YOU! You are the Master cutter of your life. There are millions of diamonds available, but there's only one like YOU. So take responsibility and take control. Map out what you want your life to be, take the initial step, monitor the process, balance out all your facets, receive the Divine Light, and show the world your magnificent brilliance.

Introduction

It all started with a simple question. One day I was in the middle of a sales presentation when an unexpected question suddenly came to mind. I ignored this question and figured I could always address it later after I finished up the sale I was determined to complete. This presentation was for a diamond engagement ring. While I was filling out and finalizing the paperwork, the client asked me;

"You must feel really good after each sale you make?"

I replied with a smile;

"Why do you ask this question?"

"Well, you look like you love what you do. You explained this diamond thing to me like it was second nature, and you have so much passion!"

After my head and ego inflated to the size of Manhattan, I answered him with my red face;

"Thank you. You are too kind"

"No, no, I'm serious!" he said. *"You must feel really fulfilled every time you share your knowledge and passion with people."*

I paused there for a moment, and my eyes went blank. I could not hear anything, and in that split second, it felt as if time had stopped.

"Yes, you're right. I do feel very fulfilled."

As I was speaking, I realized that this man was talking to me from a completely different level or dimension. He was referring to the question I was just asking myself. Did I pick up his thoughts before he asked the question? Or did he pick up mine somehow? I didn't know. One thing I did know for sure was that I loved diamonds. I loved selling diamonds. I loved everything about diamonds. I loved helping people select their diamond as I understood their meaning. I loved talking about diamonds, and I talked about them all the time. But did selling diamonds really fulfill me? I realized that I had been asking myself this question subconsciously for a while, and on that day this question surfaced and became conscious. This question has a two-part answer. The first one is yes, I did feel very fulfilled. Come to think of it, it's actually an honor to be in this position. Think about it for a moment. To this day, I get to help a person select the symbol of his or her love for another person with whom he or she has chosen to spend the rest of his or her life. This ring, this diamond is going to be the symbol of their union. They will always remember when and where they got it. He's certainly going to remember how much he spent on it since it is very strange for most men to spend money on things like jewelry and diamonds. He's certainly going to remember the experience he had when he bought it. You see, most jewelry salespeople don't understand that the experience they give to their clients is the single most important part of their presentation. I feel amazing spending time with someone new and sharing my passion. This is a mysterious crystal that most people know so little or nothing about, but yet they are willing to spend crazy amounts of money to own one. It's probably one of the smallest but most expensive items created by Mother Nature. (Let's leave uranium and plutonium out of this please!) Yet it is the single most emotionally charged gift a human being can give to another human. I have seen women getting more excited when receiving a diamond than some other women getting Mercedes-Benz! It's mind-boggling! What's going on here? How could this be possible? It's just a diamond, a tiny shiny crystal that can bring so much joy and happiness in people's lives. So it truly is an honor and a privilege to help someone with this occasion. You know the good old saying, "Diamonds are a girl's best friend!" You've heard that song a few times, haven't you? Well, diamonds are my best friends too.

The first part of the answer is yes. What's the second part? The second part was a part that I could only get answered if I asked a second question. My client was still in front of me, talking away. I said to him;

"How are you going to propose?"

I feel that as part of my job as a diamond consultant, it is my responsibility to help each and every client with the proposal stage. Obviously, I'm not going to play the cello or start singing in Italian while he's on his knees, crying his eyes out, trying to read a poem he spent two weeks writing and rehearsing, and begging her to marry him. No, I won't do that! (here's another song). I mean helping him trigger some ideas in his mind by asking a series of questions. I call them my "4C's" questions. Okay, I know what you are thinking!

It's sounds corny, and this 4C's thing is overused. But it really helps. Trust me on this one. Can you guess what the C stand for? Not in this particular order, the first "C" stands for "What to do." The second is "Where to go." The third "When to do it." And the last is "What to say." So what do the 4C's have to do with this? None of these questions start with the letter C. Some people told me it should be called the 4W's. Well, it can be if that works for you, but the C's stand for Challenge. Why challenge? It's simple. In my many years in the industry, I have come to realize that most men have a real challenge with finding answers to these simple questions. The truth is that most men are romantically challenged. Hence, the "C." Lo and behold, the gentleman left very content with his purchase, and the day continued.

I didn't know what the second question was until a few weeks later. When I arrived home, I was feeling a little down. I had just realized that what I was doing wasn't totally fulfilling me. I was in a state of doubt about my work and even my career. I started asking myself a bunch of questions; however, it seemed like they led me in an endless loop questions, and none was helping me move past these feelings. Nothing made any sense. I went to bed, hoping that these back and forth questions/answers thing would go away in my sleep and that I would wake up next day without thinking about it. Luckily, I woke up the next morning, and they were gone. I was back on the bus on my way to Manhattan, excited as can be about my diamonds and meeting new people.

Some time went by, and I had completely forgotten about that experience with that client—that is, until it happened again with new client;

"You must feel really fulfilled! You have so much passion! You are so lucky to have found your passion and do what you love most... Blah, blah, blah!"

When I went home that evening, I had to find this second part of my question, and out of frustration came this;

"What is it about diamonds that I'm so passionate about?"

I already knew diamonds fascinated me, so I asked another question;

"What is it about diamonds that fascinates me so much?"

This question really opened up something bigger than I could have ever imagined at that time. And I said out loud;

"Yeah, what is it that's so fascinating to me about diamonds?" I guess I was lucky to know that I was at least in the right industry.

Flashback: Spring Valley, April 1992

I'll never forget an event that happened to me when I was eighteen years old. I was working with my parents at a jewelry exchange upstate New York in small city called Spring Valley. This was at the very beginning of my career prior to Manhattan. My father had an opportunity to open a booth in that place to sale and repair jewelry at the retail level. I had just graduated high school and turned seventeen. I like to study, but I was never a big school person and could not sit still for more than three minutes studying a topic I didn't really care about. While in high school around graduation time, I wasn't sure if I wanted to continue school and go to college. I was working as a stock boy for about a year and half at a local stationary store called Drapkin's in Ridgewood, New Jersey, where I lived, and I was making a decent amount of money for a high school kid. So my father came to me one day and asked me;

"How much longer are you going to take out the trash, vacuum the carpet, mop the floor, and assemble the newspapers on Sundays for that store?"

(Different sections of various Sunday newspapers arrived on different days during the week and someone had to put them together and get them ready for the Sunday morning newspaper rush in the store.)

I answered him with a little delay;

"Why do you ask?" And I knew where this was going, so I continued, *"I have no intention of sitting at a bench and setting stones and soldering pieces of metal together all day long."*

He said;

"I have an opportunity to open a retail booth and sell jewelry and diamonds. You would be good at selling jewelry there. You have a way with people, and you can learn a trade just like I did when I was your age."

To be frank, I did not want to go to college yet. Somehow, I did not think it was the right path for me. But I have always been an open-minded person, so I figured, what the heck? Maybe my father was right. I could learn a trade, and he would be my guide and teach me the tricks and secrets of the trade. So I welcomed the opportunity with open arms and jumped right into it. It was the beginning of the summer 1991, and I was just turning seventeen.

It wasn't long until I realized that I was very lucky. I had a father to teach me the tricks of manufacturing. There were other professionals all around me, and I knew I could learn from them too. I was also very young and full of energy. So I grabbed books and trade publications and articles and started reading, feeding my mind constantly with information. I remember very clearly saying to myself that I needed to keep my ears and eyes wide open and open my mouth only to ask productive and constructive questions. And besides, my English was very limited at the time, so it was a great excuse to keep my mouth shut. One of the things I have learned and relearned from sales professionals over my years in selling is that there is a good reason why we all have two ears and one mouth. We should listen twice as much as we talk. Great analogy!

I enrolled in a home study program through GIA (Gemological Institute of America) and started my first course on diamonds. I was even luckier to have my father as the point person for diamond setting in the entire exchange, which gave me the opportunity to examine every single diamond that he set. The opportunity was perfect. I graded diamonds day in and day out. I even asked the other jewelers to bring the diamonds to us without the parcel papers, which usually have the carat weight, the color and the clarity of the stone, and even sometimes all the measurements angles and percentages, so that I could test myself. I got to see and examine a large variety of diamonds on a daily basis. I grabbed every single diamond I could get my tweezers on and dissected them with my loupe, constantly testing my grading abilities and myself. My accuracy was sharpening very rapidly until pretty soon I was right on 99 percent of the time.

A year went by, and on a slow Wednesday morning, one of the jewelers came to our booth with a loose stone in one hand and a ring on the other. He looked at me and said;

"Yvan, give this to your dad. Tell him to size the ring to a five and set the stone in. And yes, you can grade the stone."

He put the loose diamond in the palm of my left hand and waited for me to grab my tweezers and my loupe. But for the first time, I didn't. I kept the diamond in the palm of my hand, opened wide, and brought it closer to my eyes.

"Yvan, aren't you going to get your loupe and grade this stone?" And for the time I said no.

"Nick, I don't need the loupe! I can tell you right now what this stone is without the loupe." Man, did this guy laugh!

"Are you kidding me? What are you now, the diamond expert?"

I said; *"If I can grade this stone and be right on, would you consider me an expert?"*

"Yeah, right!" he replied laughing.

So I examined this small stone. It took me only a few seconds to assess a grading. I looked at him and said;

"It's obviously a Pear shape. It weighs 0.77ct. The color is G, and the clarity is VS2".

This man turned just about every color of the rainbow. With a totally astonished voice, he said;

"There's no way you could have known that! You saw the grading report! You must have seen this stone before! That's not possible!"

He went and got the grading report to validate my grading. I was right on. Both he and my father, who was sitting right next to me, couldn't believe it. To tell you the truth, I could not believe it either, but I made it look like it was a piece of cake.

"So am I an expert now?" I said with my eighteen-year-old attitude, and we all had a good laugh.

This is a story I will never forget because on that day I knew that the diamond trade was for me. I was blessed to become so good at understanding diamond grading so quickly and so early in my career. That moment was monumental for my career. Was it a lucky guess? I don't know. It was almost as if I listened to what this diamond was telling me. I could have sworn I just repeated what I heard in my mind. This occurred again and again over the years, and it always shocked everyone involved. This experience really boosted my confidence, and shortly after that, the story circulated around the entire exchange. By the way, a jewelry exchange is a large store with many booths operated and owned independently. Many jewelers started to come to me to ask for my opinion about diamonds, the ones they were selling and the ones their clients already owned.

Fast-Forward: South Beach Miami, March 2001

I was on a short vacation with some of my closest friends at the time when an unmistakably enlightening incident occurred. I was at a transition point, at a crossroad on my career path back then. Although I was doing great, I wasn't sure if I wanted to continue working in the diamond industry. I had just resigned from working with the Internet company. I had paid off all my debts, and I had saved some money, so I took a few month off to relax a little and rethink my life. What better place than Miami's beaches? At that time of my life I was very much involved as a volunteer organizer in the church youth groups, and I must say between planning sports weekends and various other activities on Sundays after church services, I had a lot of fun.

It was nice also to be able to share my personal experiences with the younger generations, I really enjoyed that. It was a form of service and contribution to the Armenian community. I was young and had a great connection with the middle school to college-age groups. I loved sharing parts of my life with them in hopes that my stories would help them with their lives. I seriously considered changing my path from diamonds to youth ministry. At that time my cousin and best friend was studying in the Armenian seminary so it seemed like it was a logical step for me to take. But deep inside, I was not convinced entirely. There was something whispering in my ear that it was not the right path to take. It was a noble path for sure, but it did not feel it was the right one for me. I didn't listen. I ignored the messages I was hearing, or I should say that I chose to ignore them to be truthful and accurate. On the other hand, I knew contributing to the community and helping the younger generation achieve better lives or at least helping them see things from a different perspective was an honorable thing to do. And it also made a lot of sense because I was close with my cousin and we always talked about helping everyone in our community. It even went as far as the Archbishop asking me to join the clergy as a youth minister. What? Me in the clergy? What? It was seen as an honor, and who could turn down such an authority figure in the church? I thought this was a blessing. I told the Archbishop I was pretty sure this was what I wanted to do, but I still wanted some time to think. He said with a convinced voice;

"Yvan, I'm looking forward to your start very soon."

In the meantime, the messages whispering in my ear were increasing. I kept hearing; *"What are you doing? Where are you going with this? Your heart isn't in it! Follow your heart! Follow your passion!"*

I continued to ignore that narrative. I wasn't sure if the whispers were products of my imagination or if they were those so-called "devilish" messages trying to get me to stay away from doing something wholesome and good—one white-winged angel with a halo on one shoulder telling me to do something and one red devil with horns and a trident on my other shoulder telling me to do the exact opposite.

It sounds funny and very Hollywood-like, but that's how it felt. Perfect example of the ego working against your inner true self. With that kind of battle raging in my mind, which was rather frustrating, I got on a plane to Miami to meet up with my friends in hopes of forgetting about this for a while. Being by the beach and in the water has always been therapeutic for me, and I thought it was what I needed to do. I stayed there for a few days with a good friend Jim who was really hospitable and let me stay at one of his houses. We went by the beach almost every day and had such a great time. The whispers got loud again and started haunting me by the last day. Knowing that I had to get back home was giving me anxiety, and hearing these whispers made me nervous. I went for one last walk on the beach before leaving when something really amazing happened. I must have walked for about half hour, maybe forty-five minutes. Frankly, I don't really know how long I walked. I realized we tend to lose track of time when we're lost in our thoughts. I believe thinking is one aspect of daydreaming, which has no real basis in our physical reality. It takes us into different dimensions, dimensions where time isn't perceived in the same way when looking at a clock. The past, the present, and the future can all be experienced at the same time. It's also known as the *Now*. But that's an entirely different conversation that perhaps we can have at another time. Some time passed before I got back to the spot where all my friends were laying out. During that time I tried to focus on these whispers. But again, how would I know if they were real? How would I know that they weren't some imaginary trick I was playing on myself? I was so disheartened, so frustrated, so disappointed with myself, and so confused that I looked up in the sky and said very loudly;

"Please give me a sign! Show me something I can be sure of. What is my path? What am I supposed to do?"

I really wanted a real sign, not just confusing whispers. I wanted something concrete, something that would tell me exactly what to do. I opened my arms and my face to the sky as if I was waiting for something to fall into my arms. I just hoped it wasn't going to be a lightning bolt!! Then my arms went from an up position to down. I had my face down looking at my feet as they were slowing submerged by the waves, right foot first and then the left. My feet were getting covered with sand as they slowly sank and soon completely covered. I felt as if I couldn't move or maybe didn't want to. Going back to my friends meant going back home shortly after, and I knew making a decision was eminent. I had such a disappointed and desperate look on my face. I knew exactly where I was standing, yet I felt so lost. I looked up to see how far away my friends were. They were just about a hundred feet away. As I was standing in the same spot, looking straight ahead, my vision got blurry. The ocean and people around me sounded as if they were all in a tube and soon became one big blend of blurry noises. At that precise moment, something caught my left eye. There was something shiny in my peripheral vision to my lower left side. That shimmer pierced right through that blur like the first sunlight piercing through the morning fog. I thought it must be a bottle cap or a piece of glass. But at the same time, I thought glass on the beach didn't shine because of tumbling in the sand—that is, unless it had just been broken. I turned my head toward it and took half of a step and leaned over to see what this glimmering object could be. I was so lost in my thoughts that I did not believe what I was looking at. I refused to believe it. I looked up at the sky and said;

"Are you kidding me? You've got to be kidding me, right?"

I put my hands on my face, rubbed my eyes, and looked down again. This time I knelt down and picked up this object before the waves covered it up. It was a diamond. A one-carat, fully faceted, round diamond! In the palm of my left hand, I held a loose diamond. It was at the exact spot where I had stopped a few seconds before and asked for a concrete sign about which path I should take, and there was a diamond. That's impossible! There was no way this could be happening to me. What were the chances for this to occur? I thought, what are the odds? I found a loose diamond in the sand on a beach seconds after asking the universe for answers or a concrete sign. I got an answer practically instantly. Thank God I didn't ask for that lightning bolt, I would have had a completely different perceptive on the Diving Light! I was disoriented and uncertain of my career path. I didn't know if I should stay in the jewelry business or seek another career. Knowing diamonds very well, I took a better look at the crystal in my hand. It was indeed the size of a one-carat diamond. It was white and clear, fully faceted, and very shiny just like a diamond. But it turned out to be a CZ, a cubic zirconia. What the heck was a loose CZ doing on the beach right at the spot where I had stopped? But that was beside the point. I had asked for a sign, and I had gotten one instantly. It didn't matter whether it was a real diamond or not, it still represented a diamond. To this day, I still have it. I set it inside a miniature gold loupe charm pendant I made. Every time I look at it, I think of that moment when I found it. I think that regardless of where we are in our lives, regardless of where we stand, literally in my case on a beach far away from home, the Divine Light is always present, always around at any given time, even if you don't see it or feel it or hear it. The Light works in mysterious ways. This brings me to another point, and that is the principle of omnipresence. We can make a parallel between diamonds and humans. The light that enters the diamond is reflected in all directions, not just toward the observer. The reflections inside the diamond and our internal world are the same; if perfect balance is attained inside the diamond

                                    Yvan Kaprielian

then perfect reflection and perfect balance will be attained outside the diamond. This is the same for us human beings. What we see and experience outside of ourselves, our external world, is a direct reflection of what is being experienced inside of ourselves, our internal world. The way we see ourselves is the way we see the world. It's all about reflection. I told you these stories so that you could understand why I had to ask these questions and why I really needed answers. At that point seventeen years had now gone by since I first set foot into the diamond industry. I've had the special privileges to meet and work with great experts and professionals. I've had the priceless experience to manufacture diamond jewelry myself. I've had the opportunity to help and guide people in making one of the most significant purchases of their lives. Some I never even saw or met in person as I was selling diamonds for an Internet company at one point. Diamonds have always been a big part of my life. I can't imagine myself without diamonds around me. But why so much experience? Why did I work in so many different aspect of this industry? Why did I go from retail sales to manufacturing and wholesaling to selling diamonds online to building diamond databases and search engines for internet companies to leading selling seminars and educational programs for the trade and for consumers? And why did I get back into retail sales again after being away from it for a while? In the summer of 2005, I finally got my answer. The answer came to me in the form of an epiphany, an amazing realization. I believe I had to be exposed to all these different aspects—or shall I say *facets*? —of the diamond industry to understand that diamonds were far more than mere symbols of engagements or anniversaries. They are, in fact, symbols of our lives. I strongly believe that diamonds are an exact representation of our lives. Diamonds are messages from Mother Earth to human beings. But that's just the tip of the iceberg.

Chapter I

The Formation

"On the way up"

Some ancient legends and myths say that diamonds are splinters of the stars that fell onto the earth. Others say that they are frozen tears from the Gods. Others argue that diamonds have an eternal fire inside them that no one could snuff out no matter what they tried. Some legends say that when men tried to break them with an axe or hammer, either the tool or the anvil that would break while the diamond remained intact. There are many legends like these illustrating that diamonds have always been a mystery. The actual root of the word *diamond* comes from the Greek word *adamas*, which means unconquerable, unbreakable, or invincible. Diamonds are formed deep inside the earth somewhere between 125 to 175 miles below the surface. That's the only depth with adequate pressure and temperature for them to form. Once formed, diamonds are brought closer to the surface through various types of volcanic eruptions, which is when they can complete their crystallization journey. Over millions of years, diamonds can travel down old and extinct volcanoes by the process of erosion and make their way into streams and riverbeds. The diamonds found in the rivers are called *alluvial deposit diamonds*. The ones that have remained in volcanic pipes are called *kimberlite deposit diamonds*. A kimberlite pipe is a carrot-shaped pipe that is formed by the pressure of the magma being pushed up to the surface of the earth. There are many types of mines and mining techniques to extract diamonds. We'll get to that in the next chapter.

Diamonds must be very strong, as they have to endure harsh environments, pressure, and heat from all around in order to reach the surface. They could wait a long time—tens and hundreds of thousands of years perhaps—before they have an opportunity to emerge and see the light. Sometimes if the conditions are favorable, they can reach daylight in a fast and more sudden manner, such as a volcanic eruption or explosion.

We can parallel our lives in the same respect. You may think sometimes we need to wait a long time before an opportunity to see the light emerges, sometimes it could be abrupt. I'm sure you've heard the phrase "There is light at the end of the tunnel." From the center of the earth, the magma is pushed up with immeasurable power and force, bringing diamonds to the surface. It is the same for us. With the power and force of our emotions combined with willpower, we can move through some really rough times and turmoil—whether with the emotions of pain and suffering, anger and sadness. Or love, joy, happiness, compassion, and selflessness. These are emotions that push us to the surface where there's light … at the end of the tunnel. We must be strong emotionally, mentally, and physically to sustain harsh environments and all sorts of pressure to survive. Sudden volcanic eruptions can be related to human epiphanies emerging out of seemingly nowhere into our conscious awareness, many times represented in today's society as the light bulb above one's head. That moment does not always have to feel like an emotional earthquake. Instead it could be that time when we let go of a certain desire for an answer. All of a sudden, the answer just shows up. It's that *eureka,* the *"aha"* moment. What actually happens is that we get out of our own way. Our own mind often takes us to places where the answer isn't present. Therefore, we end up focusing on everything but the answer. The answer can also be related to those moments when we reach the point of absolute frustration and we say to ourselves, "That's it! I've had it. No more of this life. I want better. I want more." We can feel an explosion of emotions deep inside that pushes us to make decisions and take drastic actions toward new horizons to improve ourselves and increase the quality of our lives. And sometimes we have to wait a longer period of time before we realize that we are stuck. For a diamond this event most likely only happens once in its life span, but for most of us humans, this is a process that may repeat itself many times over in our lifetime. This is true for me as I've been stuck many times in my life, not knowing what to do or if I should even do something about a situation. There's a fine line between being comfortable and stuck. Which is it? Am I stuck, or am I comfortable? So I've tried to always look at these times as a necessity—the moments in my life I needed to experience and go through in order to realize that I was hungry for more and for better things. Or perhaps it was time to pick my *"stuff"* up and keep moving. My spiritual teacher always said that the most important thing is that you keep moving forward. The rough times as well as the good times are just temporary, but you need to always keep moving forward and improve your development. The more you practice self-improvement and self-development, the less likely you linger around in a *stuck* state. Once I had taken a thorough look around to see where I was in the many facets of my life, making a decision wasn't complicated. I easily made the decision to *dislodge* myself from being stuck and make an upward move in my life. Just like a diamond, we need to keep moving up and reach higher grounds. So here are a few simple questions for you. Where are you in the many facets of your life? Are you stuck, or are you moving upward? Where would you like your life to be? Simple questions can change the quality of your life. But we have to ask the right questions to get quality answers.

Chapter II
Mining

"The journey until it is found"

Let's talk about mining diamonds. The process of digging diamonds out of the ground is very laborious, lengthy, and can be a dangerous business. Sometimes, if not all the time, the conditions in which miners work can be treacherous, and can put their lives at risk. Diamonds are often mined in extreme temperatures way outside of what most of us have ever experienced in our lifetime. They are also mined in areas so remote from any type of society that miners are often on a site for months, sometimes years before returning to communities and societies as we know them. They are also paid very low wages and work hard and long hours. As a side note, this is true for other gemstones, minerals, and metals around the world, as many mining techniques will apply just the same. Don't think that only diamonds are mined this way. Mining techniques are adjusted and adapted to their respective terrains and locations. There are places in the world where miners are under tremendous pressure, and a lot of the times, they have to work in poor conditions like hot temperatures. They may have to endure humidity and diseases, and they may work in virus-infected areas and experience conditions that are detrimental to their health. Many of the countries where diamonds and other gemstones are mined suffer from major poverty and remain under constant harassment from the governments, locals, and mine owners. Sometimes mines can be controlled by people with bad intentions and diamonds and other gemstones are smuggled out of these countries and used as monetary exchange for weapons. They may even fund violent rebel movements throughout the world. Those diamonds are called *conflict* or *blood diamonds*. How can people do this? How can diamonds and gemstones be used to destroy on one side of the world and to create and celebrate new marriages or anniversaries or birthdays on another side of the world? I could not understand it. If misused, something so magnificent and so pure could be so dangerous. This was true in the past, and thank God that nowadays the mining process is closely and legally monitored and controlled. In reality, the conflict diamonds represented a fraction of a percent of the world's production, and if they did slip through the cracks, they were rough and uncut. A process called the Kimberley Process was put in place in 2003, and the World Diamond Council is very strict and monitors diamond transactions closely from the mine to the counter. Heavy sanctions are pressed upon companies that don't comply with the rules. Most large diamond companies, retailers, and wholesalers now certify their diamonds and their source of origin as being conflict-free. Although most retailers will not give you an actual conflict-free certification, rest assured that their suppliers have basically no choice but to comply, or they will face heavy sanctions and perhaps even be forced to close their doors altogether. This is mainly because the council will demand compliance, but retailers demand it as well. End consumers such as yourself want to make sure they are purchasing a fair-trade product. I'm with you 100%.

As I meditated on that for a while, the answer became obvious. People would do anything to get their hands on diamonds. They would go to great distances and to extreme extents to seek and find diamonds because of the monetary value. They go as far as killing one another. Making the parallel once again, digging for diamonds in mines is nothing more than just a representation of what humans should really be doing. Instead of looking for ways to dig bigger and deeper holes in the ground in order to look for diamonds, they should find better ways to dig deeper in their heads and look for better way to live and better ways to manifest their dreams and desires. The true diamond mine is in our mind and in our Soul. Without exceptions, we all have diamonds in our mind. We are the diamond mines, and we have a diamond mind. A great book to read is *Acres of Diamonds* by Russell Conwell, in which he tells the story of a farmer who sold everything he owned including his land and home and went on the quest for diamonds only to realize that he was sitting on one the entire time. Instead of looking for diamonds in some remote and hostile place, we need to look within ourselves. That's where the real valuable diamonds are. We are constantly producing thoughts and ideas that are truly magnificent diamonds just waiting to be cut, faceted, and radiate their brilliance. Money, power, and fame are just external gains that people seek in order to justify their external world, their external needs. However, in reality, just like a diamond, true beauty and brilliance comes from within.

He who looks outside, dreams.

He who looks inside, awakens.

- Carl Gustave Jung -

Keeping that in mind, just think about how many amazing inventions have come to life in last fifty years. Think about how many have come to life in the past two hundred years and beyond. And how many do you think will come to life in the future? They are countless, and they all came from someone's diamond mind/mine. Not all great inventions were perfect at first. Just like a diamond, they had to be cut and faceted and polished over again until it was perfect, until it reached its maximum potential, its maximum brilliance. Speaking of light and inventions, it is said that Thomas Edison tried ten thousand times before he made the first working light bulb. My spiritual teacher, Grand Master

Choa Kok Sui, is the founder of Modern Pranic Healing and Arhatic Yoga. He is now internationally recognized as the one of the most advanced experts on no-touch energy healing in the world. He revolutionized energy healing modalities and today Pranic Healing is the fastest growing energy healing modality. How do you think he formulated all this? He didn't wake up one day and just master energy healing. It took years of practice, testing, experimenting, and evaluating. How many times are you willing to try to be more brilliant before you give up?

Different Mines, Different Minds

They are many various ways to recover diamonds from Mother Earth. Diamonds can be found all around the world, although there are places that yield more than others. Some of these places include (not in order of production) most of Southern Africa, such as Sierra Leone and the Ivory Coast and surrounding countries, Australia, Northern Russia, Canada, India, Brazil, Venezuela, and some parts of China. You can even find some in the United States but in very small quantities, and most are not gem quality, which means they are used mostly for industrial purposes. Although some jewelry designers have emerged over the years and found creative ways to produce quality and beautiful designs with those rough diamonds. The most popular diamond found in the United States was in Crater of Diamonds Park, Arkansas in 1924. It's called "Uncle Sam," and it originally weighed 40.23ct in the rough.

Uncle Sam Diamond. Photo Courtesy of GIA

(Gemological Institute of America)

Alluvial Deposit Mining

This is the oldest form of mining for diamonds, gemstones, and precious metals. Nature's treasures are found in existing rivers or dried-out riverbeds. Over millions of years as the earth changed landscapes, oceans and rivers have moved, leaving exposed minerals, gems, and precious metal within old ocean floors and riverbeds. By the natural process of erosion, the gems have tumbled down streams from higher places, bringing down along with them a portion of these treasures. Some of them have remained in their place, perhaps because of the depth at which they were stuck after they were pushed up from deeper underground. This leads to other type of mining, and I'll describe them in the next a few pages.

It is said that some of the more pure diamonds— as far as clarity is concerned—are found in alluvial deposits. Although there's no actual evidence, this could be due to the endless tumbling against other materials going downstream. It is a natural selection of the strongest. Diamonds with heavier inclusions and blemishes may not be able to sustain the intensity of the tumbling and could disintegrate over time. The tools required for this type of mining are very basic. All you'll need is a pan, a shovel, and a strong back. You might have heard of the gold rush of the 1850s. People were panning for gold in the rivers out west in California, and they were using this same technique. Sometimes for old dried-out riverbeds, they have to bring in water and create canals so that they could use the panning method. The basic idea is to sort out dirt from larger materials and select what they are looking for. It's much easier for gold since it's probably one of the only natural mineral that's a true glowing and majestic yellow. However, it can be trickier for diamonds. Not all diamonds are crystal clear when found. They could like your average gravel or tiny pebble. Their shape too can be a challenge to recognize and differentiate among other rocks and stones. The best-looking, well-formed rough diamond is in a shape called octahedron. It's basically two four-sided pyramid base to base.

Photo courtesy of GIA (Gemological Institute of America)

However, because of various pressures and temperatures, crystal structure distortions can take place, and diamonds can form in many different shapes. Take a look at the image.

Yvan Kaprielian

Photo courtesy of IGI (International Gemological Institute)

When technology allowed, they were able to divert rivers from their natural course and go to the bottom of now dried and exposed riverbeds and search for diamonds and other minerals. It's an interesting and intelligent process!

Open Pit Mining

This type of mining consists of digging big and deep holes in the ground where the Kimberlite pipe is found. These big pits are shaped like inverted cones and can be very deep. One of the most well-known mine is located in Siberia and called the Mir Mine, 525 meters (1,725 feet) deep and 1,200 meters (3,940 feet) across, just about three-quarters of a mile wide or eighty-nine acres in surface.

To give you a perspective and a visual point of reference, the Jacqueline Kennedy Onassis Reservoir in Central Park is 106 acres. So that mine is about three-quarters of the entire surface of the reservoir. If you've never been in NYC, this is one the many good reasons to come visit. The images are not exactly to scale in comparison, but it's close. The mine opened in 1957 during an extremely cold climate. Winters lasted from seven to eight months, and temperatures would drop to the point where gasoline would freeze and rubber tires would shatter like glass. Mining was virtually impossible. During the summer months, permafrost ground would warm up and partially melt, leaving the surface muddy and slippery and making mining another challenge. Even some of the nearby buildings had to be lifted so that they would not sink. A town of nearly thirty-seven thousand people was built on its precipice. Trucks would drive up and down the pit in a spiral manner. The ore processing plant was eighteen miles away on more stable ground. During its peak producing years, the mine yielded some ten million carats of rough diamonds per year with an average of 20% being of gem quality that was suitable for jewelry. The rest were industrial-grade. Generally, if the mine is large enough, open-pit mines are accompanied with underground tunneling operations. Mir was one of them.

Yvan Kaprielian

In order to have one carat of rough diamonds, on average some twenty to twenty-five tons of ore had to be processed. You might ask, "How do they actually find diamonds in the millions of tons of ore they extract form the mines?" Well, that's a great question. From the mine shafts and truckloads, the ore is transported via conveyer belts to the sorting stations. There, the ore is separated—rocks on one side and loose dirt on another. The larger rocks are crushed in gigantic super-powerful machines to reach a desired size. The loose ore and dirt is sifted with water, and rocks and gravel are separated. They all end up in the same place for sorting. One way to separate diamonds from other ground materials and stones is to pass them through what is called a grease table. These are covered with a thick layer of grease. These tables either spin and use centrifugal force for separation, or they jump and thrust up and back down fast, making the materials jump up and down in a forward motion, much like jumping beans. Why grease? Diamonds and grease are great friends. They stick together! Diamonds don't get "*wet*" like other materials tend to, and they stick to grease more readily. They have a surface that looks and feels waxy as if you just finished waxing and polishing the hood of your car. It looks like the water can't stay on the paint and beads right off. That's similar for the surface of a diamond. Didn't you ever wonder why your diamonds always look dirty and oily even after your jeweler gave it a good cleaning the day before? This is why. Water from your skin evaporates and takes along with it natural body oil and get stuck on your diamond in a process called condensation. Of course, that's assuming you didn't put hand lotion all over your rings like I've seen so many women do and wonder why their rings were always dirty. Then, once it's greasy and oily, more *stuff* gets stuck to it like lint and fabric fiber from clothing, soap residue, dust in the air, and others, and makes it even dirtier. It's a never-ending cycle. It's a natural phenomenon. You can't go around it. People would come back to me after a week and say;

"I don't understand. You cleaned my ring a few days ago, and it's dirty again. Why?"

So don't worry. It's normal. By the way, I just demystify that enigma for you. Most people, even individuals in our industry don't understand this.

There's a story called "The Legend of the Valley of Diamonds" in India that was started at the time of Alexander the Great around 335 BC. The story is told again in Marco Polo's voyages going back to thirteenth century AD. It's the legend of a valley in India where diamonds were literally carpeting the ground, at hands reach, for anyone to collect. However, the valley was protected by giant venomous and deadly snakes and virtually impenetrable on foot. The only way was by air. Alexander had heard of the story of Sinbad the sailor, who tied himself to the leg of a giant eagle and flew in a cave right near the diamondiferous valley. There, he saw that some people at the valley tops would throw big pieces of greasy meat down the valley to get the diamonds. The diamonds would stick to the greasy meat, and the eagles would go get the meat to bring back to their nest to feed their young, unaware they were doing these people a huge favor. Afterward, the merchants would go to the nest and collect the diamonds. This is a simplified version of the legend, but the idea is there.

So the table either spins or jumps, and materials other than

diamonds are moved away. This is an old technique still

                                                    Yvan Kaprielian

used today. However, it has been enhanced and improved by more modern technology from the twenty first century.

There are many ways to find ideas and make changes in your life. Some may be right under your nose and may require only minimal work, and some may require some serious digging. Sometimes less is best. The Hope Diamond was discovered in an alluvial deposit, a few feet just below the surface. Today it is known to be one of the most valued and also the most famous diamonds in the world. Want to know why I'm telling you this? You have no idea how good things could turn out. If you research the story of the Hope Diamond, what you'll find it amazing. Well, you won't have to. I've done that for you. I've had the opportunity to see many amazing diamonds over the years, but I must say that this is one of the most magnificent diamonds I have ever seen. The evenness and depth of color, not to mention the shape and particularly the size for such color, it is absolutely fascinating. The diamond originated from the Golconda mine in India in the early 1600s, which at the time was the only significant known source of diamonds. In 1668, a famous French traveler and gem merchant named Jean

Baptiste Tavernier sold the blue diamond to the Sun King Louis XIV, king of France.

The diamond weighed about 112ct and was polished with a few facets. In 1673, Louis XIV had the gem recut and polished to increase its beauty and brilliant, but it was reduced to 67.5ct. It was then mounted as a pendant and became part of the Crown Jewels of France, in which it remained until 1749, when the king's successor, Louis the XV, had it remounted in a piece of ceremonial jewelry called the Emblem of the Golden Fleece. In 1792, the French Blue was stolen during a looting associated with the French Revolution, which erupted during the reign of Louis XVI and his queen, Marie Antoinette. The diamond disappeared and was unheard of for some twenty years. Interestingly, in 1812, a large blue diamond emerged out of nowhere in London. It was smaller by about 20ct. Some evidence has been found that the French Blue was recut and reduced in size to about 45ct and was sold to the king of England, George IV. A banker and gem collector named Henry Phillip Hope bought the diamond after the king's death in 1830. From this point on, the diamond bore the

                                   Yvan Kaprielian

name Hope. It remained in the Hope family until 1901, at which time it was sold back and forth between merchants and collectors in London, New York, and Paris. In 1909, Pierre Cartier bought it at an auction and mounted it in the necklace in which it currently is displayed. Evalyn Walsh McLean, wife of the former owner of the Washington Post, Ned McLean, bought it from Cartier in 1911 for $180,000.

Just to let you know, she also acquired the "Star of the East" diamond, a magnificent 94.8ct colorless pear-shaped diamond from Cartier the year before as a wedding gift from her father. Mrs. McLean contributed greatly to the

Yvan Kaprielian

legend of the Hope Diamond. She wore it everywhere and loved telling stories about it. She even pawned the diamond to get fast cash to help pay off the ransom of $50,000 for Charles and Anne Morrow Lindberg's baby boy's kidnapping in 1932. Charles Lindberg was the first pilot to cross the Atlantic in the single-engine airplane, the *Spirit of Saint Louis*, on May 21, 1927. It's so interesting to see how some of these stories are interrelated to one another. Two years later in 1947, after Evalyn Walsh McLean's passing, the prominent New York jeweler Harry Winston bought her entire collection of jewelry. For nine years the Hope Diamond traveled the country under the blinding flashlights of reporters, journalists, and storytellers. Finally, on November 10, 1958, the Hope Diamond was donated by Mr. Winston to the Smithsonian Institution. In 1996, the Hope Diamond was graded by the Gemological Institute of America (GIA) as an asymmetrical Cushion Antique Brilliant with fifty-eight facets, weighing 45.52ct and as an intense fancy, dark grayish blue and VS1 clarity. The diamond also displays amazing orange-red phosphorescence, a characteristic that is almost exclusively limited to dark blue diamonds, but its intensity is as rare as the diamond itself. It is surrounded with sixteen white antique cushion-shaped diamonds and forty-six more on the chain. To give you an idea of the size, it's about the size of a walnut. It's estimated to be worth $350 million. Pocket change!

Who knew such a story would arise from this diamond from such a long time ago. You just never know how good things could turn out! Either way, you will have some sorting out to do. Everything is a process. The good thing is that if you know the nature of what you are looking for, you can use the right tools and the right strategy to simplify the process. But the key is to start and never underestimate the value of your ideas, no matter how small and insignificant they may appear at the beginning. If you think of the moment when you reached a particular goal, ask yourself this question: "How did I get here?" Or if you're in a place in your life where you're not happy, ask yourself the same question: "How did I get here?" If you're honest with yourself and take full responsibility for your each and every thoughts and actions, you might realize it all might have started with something seemingly insignificant. So next time you set out to accomplish a new goal, understand that each and every one of your thoughts and actions are important, even if they seem miniscule or insignificant at the time.

NOTES

Chapter III
The Cutting

The cutting process has evolved dramatically in the past century. Computerized systems and machines have been invented to maximize time and efficiency, improve brilliance, and minimize weight loss from the original rough.

So what is the first step? The first step is the planning of the cut. The cutter usually polishes a small facet or window right on the rough diamond in order to see what's inside it. This is an important initial step because he needs to determine where the clarity characteristics are located, what their nature is, what size they are, and how many there are, if any. Once this is determined, he starts planning what the shape it will ultimately be. The cutter starts to plan each and every facet and how he will arrange and position them on the diamond. Is it going to be round, square, oval, emerald-cut, or marquis? This initial step requires a lot of time. It is very important to know what direction he needs to go because he's going to get only one shot at cutting it the best possible way. This is extremely important for the larger rough diamonds. He needs to figure out the right ratio between the shape and carat weight in order to get the most and best out of the rough. If the facets are not well aligned with one another, it will have a negative effect on brilliance. Alignment is critical. Moreover, if the cutter needs to start over, he can lose a great amount of time and rough material, which ultimately reduces the value of the finished gem.

For some diamonds that are internationally known, because of their size and rare attributes, it took more than a year of planning before the diamond went anywhere near the cutting station. One famous diamond called the DeBeers Centenary Diamond, which was cut by Gabriel Tolkowsky, weighs 273.85ct, making it the largest flawless modern-cut diamond in the world. The task took three years.

The planning is what determines every step of the cutting process just like an architect draws up the blueprints for a building to determine the location of every window, doorway, wall, water pipes etc... Imagine a house built without blueprints. Do you think some things might end up being a little off? Like a crooked doorway for example or a staircase that is not straight. Or perhaps the walls are not perpendicular to the floor or the ceiling is a little higher on one side. Can you imagine yourself in a house like that? Unless you enjoy abstract architecture, it would probably not be very attractive. It likely won't have as much value, and if you were the real estate agent, you would probably have a hard time convincing a prospect that it is a sound investment. The same goes for a diamond. There are many diamonds out there that are not cut properly. Not all diamonds have perfectly aligned facets, perfectly centered culet, or the correct amount of facets for their respective shape.

Speaking of alignment let me share with you a very important part of my learning experience on this topic. In 1996, I got into a car accident. I was driving peacefully when another driver decided to switch lanes right behind me as the traffic light was turning red. She probably didn't realize I was slowing down and rear-ended my car. I don't remember how fast we were going, maybe fifteen to twenty miles per hour at the time of the hit. The impact didn't feel that hard at all. I was lucky. When I came home that day, I called my friend Sue to tell her about it. She, being more wise than me, said I should really consider seeing a doctor and that being impacted from the back in a car crash could lead to you developing problems in the neck years later, long after you had forgotten about that accident. She insisted I go see her chiropractic specialist. I was very stubborn, but I didn't want to argue with her, so I agreed to go. When I arrived at the office, I said;

"Hey, Doc, I'm a tough guy, and I don't think I need this stuff. But my friend Sue—she's also your patient—forced me to come see you. So here I am. Let's make it quick!"

His name was Dr. Goodmark. He said with a smile, *"That's great. I'm happy to meet you too. Step into my office."*

After I explained to him the circumstances, he wanted to check the basics first and asked me to step up on a machine with two small square platforms— one for the right foot and one for the left foot. These platforms were independently operated. They would go up or down according to the test. Then he placed another device on my hips, tightly on my lower back, and the top part of my hip bones. Then with a foot-operated lever, he started rising the right foot platform. It felt really strange, to the point where I felt my right hip was significantly higher than the left side. He said;

"How does that feel?"

"It feels weird. My right side is a lot higher than my left side," I replied.

"Great observation. Your hips are actually aligned now."

Little did I know that the device on my hips and lower back had a bubble level. He pumped up the right platform until that bubble was leveled. Then he said with a smile;

"Your right hip if off alignment from your left by three-quarters of inch, tough guy!"

It turns out that there was nothing wrong with my neck, but my lower back needed attention. Was that due to the accident? I don't know. I didn't think so, and I didn't care. I wanted that problem fixed. I ended up going back to see him for adjustments three times a week for the first month and slowly winding the therapy down until my body held the adjustments. And every time I went, he taught me something new about the human skeleton structure, the spine, the vertebras, the spinal cord, and the nervous system. I learned what subluxation, herniated disks, and sciatica meant and all the symptoms that create back pain, even though I had no pain. He showed me ways to manipulate my body in order to relieve pain just in case in the future I had problems and could not come to see him.

He didn't just feed me a fish, he taught me how to fish.

I was twenty-two at that time, and he told me had I not come to see him to fix these issues and if I ever experienced any pain from this incident, it would most likely not manifest itself until later in my life, just like Sue had said. That resonated with me. It made complete and total sense. I went to see him on a regular basis for at least twelve years and learned so much. Through the knowledge he gave me, I was able to save myself from a major lower-back injury just about seventeen years after I had met him. I had moved to France and lived there for three years, and in October 2012, after lifting—or at least trying to lift—a very heavy piece of furniture, I threw my back out massively and herniated my L4–L5 disk. (L stands for lumber vertebrae, and each vertebrae in the lumber section of the spine are numbered.) I dropped to my knees, and I couldn't move my legs. I realized this was very bad. I was paralyzed from the waist down for almost a week, and I had massive excruciating pain shooting down both legs. I don't remember ever feeling this intense pain before. It took lots courage to push myself to get up and somehow have my girlfriend to drive me to see a doctor. The doctor immediately recommended an MRI and a surgeon's opinion. The MRI showed intense subluxation and the disk popping out on one side. As it turns out, the surgeon said;

"You need an operation. It's the only way to fix this!"

I said, *"Thanks for your opinion, Doctor. Have a great day!"*

I shook his hand and left his office, never to return. That day I decided I had to take this matter in my own hands, and so I applied what I had learned, my basic teachings from Dr. Goodmark. There was no way I was going to let a surgeon cut me open and mess around with my spine. No way! Not me! Within an hour, I found a place, something that resembled a pull-up bar where I could go and hang from my hands with my legs loose. The first time I did this, I literally felt and heard a series of loud cracks and pops from my entire spin—maybe four or five of them and a large one by the base of my spin. Any pain I had—and I'm not exaggerating here—was gone in that

                                                        Yvan Kaprielian

instant. I hung there for only fifteen seconds. Before I got up on that bar, I could barely stand straight. I had difficulty lifting my legs and walked very slowly. When I got off the bar, I could almost run. It was unbelievable. I repeated this procedure three to four times every single day for six months, even in the rain and cold. All of the pain was permanently gone within a year. You see, if you study the spin and the nervous system, you'll find that there are innumerable amount of nerves coming out of the spinal cord. The spinal cord goes through each vertebra. This is called the spinal canal. The nerves come out from the spinal cord, and these nerves reach out to virtually every part of your body. The nerves deliver electrical impulses coming from the brain. They are two-way streets, and the spinal cord is the main highway. Signals travel both ways from and to the brain in order to send and to receive information. Yes, the human body is an amazing biological machine and a very strong one. But within that strength, if it's not well taken care of, there's fragility. All it takes is the misalignment of one of these vertebras, and one or more of your nerves will be pinched. In turn, depending on the degree of misalignment and the degree of the pinch, the body will react, send information back to the brain, and let you know in form of discomfort all the way to excruciating pain, or paralysis. Pinching a nerve is like stepping on a garden hose when the water is going through it. If you've ever done this enlightening experiment when you were a kid, I'm sure you noticed that the water pressure decreased when it came out of the nozzle, depending on how hard you pressed your foot on the hose. It's same thing with the nerves and electrical impulses. But the question always remains. What do we do about it? Do we take a pill to mask the symptom? Or do we take matters in our own hands and fix the problem at the root? That surgeon wanted to cut me open and cut out a part of the disc, and I still wouldn't have any guarantee that such action would solve the problem! The only guarantee I had was, with parts cut of my disc, my body would never have the chance to properly heal on its own. Was this the only thing that this doctor could think of? That's what they teach in surgery school, and maybe that's all he knew. But I didn't think so. I didn't believe so, and I proved it. I'm not a medical doctor, and I'm not prescribing or recommending anything here. All I know is that too many times we tend to mask the problem with surgery and prescription drugs instead of fixing it at its point of origin. I refused to get the surgery, but I took matters into my own hands seconds after getting the surgeon's opinion and made a decision to heal my body on my own. I didn't feel sorry for myself and didn't let my mind to take me in a downward spiral of negative emotions and anger. Even my girlfriend tried to talk me into taking the doctors' advice. Instead, I ask myself how I had gotten here and how I could fix the problem. Within the next hour, I got up on that bar and proved it to myself and everyone around me that there was another way! Had I not done that, over a certain period of time, the discs which provide the body with flexibility would have started wearing off and thus creating irreversible erosion. The body would start to compensate for the misalignment by making changes and putting pressure on other parts of the spine in order to maintain itself at its best given the circumstances. This is how critically important alignment is! I'm speaking from my own experience, and I'm just sharing with you what worked for me.

I'm very grateful that my friend Sue pushed me to go see Dr. Goodmark. Without them, who knows what my back would have looked like today?

I told you this story because understanding alignment is absolutely critical. Everything needs a structure.

Everything needs to be in alignment in order maximize the potential.

In the case of the round diamond, which is the shape I will be referring to in this book, the correct number of facets is fifty-seven or fifty-eight. The fifty-eighth facet is the one that sometimes is present and sometimes not. Let me explain why. The culet is the point at the bottom of the stone. When it is present, it is considered a facet. When all the facets meet at the bottom of the pavilion, it forms a sharp point. It is up to the cutter's discretion to polish off that point and add a facet or to leave it pointy. Generally speaking, that facet is not even visible unless under high magnification (10x). The reason for that facet, when present, is to avoid possible chipping by the diamond setter when the stone is being mounted in a setting or to avoid possible abrasions while the stone is in a parcel with other diamonds. And yes, contrary to conventional wisdom, diamonds can chip at a sharp point. In the older style of diamond cutting, the culet was visible to the unaided eye. In 1919, Marcel Tolkowsky, the very famous master diamond cutter and uncle to Gabriel, whom I referred to earlier, mathematically calculated the best facet arrangement, angles, depth and height percentages, and facet elongation on a round diamond for optimum brilliance. Since then, this newer cutting style has been called the "Modern Round Brilliant," also referred to as the Tolkowsky Ideal or just simply the Ideal cut. Although when you research diamonds online or in stores, many companies have misused the term *Ideal*. They are expressing what their respective company considers *Ideal* to be or should be, and many times they are outside the original parameters of the true *Ideal*. It can get very confusing and frustrating. Countless times I had to explain to my clients what the differences were and undo all the misinformation they've learned from unreliable sources.

Over the years consumers have asked me why the word *Brilliant* is used and why it appears on certificates. As technology has advanced and improved, many different cutting styles have emerged. The name brilliant cut is given to diamonds that have similar facet shapes and arrangements. The Round, Oval, Marquis, Heart-shape, Pear-shape, the Princess cut (which is square), the Cushion, the Trillion (which is a triangle), and the Radiant (which is square or rectangular with cut corners) all are in the Brilliant cut family. The facets look kit-shaped or triangular. Many times I've recommended people consider the radiant for colored diamonds, particularly for fancy yellow diamonds, simply because their brilliance is noticeably lower. Therefore, they are greatly suited to display color more readily than diamonds that are really bright, such as round shape for example.

Then you have the family of the Step cuts. The most popular known is the Emerald cut, which is rectangular or square-shaped with the cut corners. The Baguette, which is most of the time rectangular or rectangular tapered and small in size, is also becoming more popular in the square shape called Carré. The Royal Asscher cut is very often mistaken for a Square Emerald cut simply because it is square. Technically, it is a Square Emerald, but it has more pronounced corners and more facets on the pavilion and on the crown than the ordinary Square Emerald cut. If you are in the jewelry business and don't know what to look for, you may easily make this mistake, and most of the time, you wouldn't even know why.

Well, this is why. Consumers out there are misled, and it drives me nuts that the great majority of the so-called jewelers don't even know the difference. I can't tell you how many people would come to see me asking about this cut with absolutely no clue what it means. That's fine, it's not their fault. They read it somewhere, and some uneducated person in the business wrote something on a topic he or she had no clue about. It's a proprietary cut and was developed in 1902 by Joseph Asscher, a famous cutter, after whom this cut was named. It is found in sizes starting at about a quarter of carat (0.25ct) and up. So why Step cut? Simply because the shape and the arrangement of the facets are like steps, trapezoid or rectangular. There's also the mix-cut family, and the most well-known example among them is the Radiant. Although it is not seen as much, it can have the pavilion cut as a Brilliant and the crown as a Step cut. And then you have all the other odd shapes such as the Kit shape, the Bullet, the Trapezoid, the Shield shape, Half Moons and a few more that are also found to be in both families. It is fascinating to me that people can cut diamonds in all these shapes. They can even cut diamonds in the shape of a Buddha, Horse heads, Fish, and Stars. Amazing!

Once you take a good look at your life, it's critical to start planning, although it could be hard to plan every step of the way like you would for a diamond. In life there are many variables and unknown factors that contribute to the development of a plan, some of which we have absolutely no control over. Everything is subjected to the law of change, so it is impossible to foresee every step and how each will unfold. Personally, I don't think our brain has that capacity in our current state of consciousness, and I don't think we are smart enough to understand or predict the inner workings of the universe. I'm speaking for myself. I don't know about you. Maybe you can, and if you do, good for you. I'd love to know how you do it. All I know is that when I achieve a goal, I go back in my mind and trace the chronology of events to understand how the process evolved. I look for turning points, where and how I got to reach my goal. All I can tell you is that no matter how detailed and meticulous my planning was, there was no way I could have known every step of the way as it unfolded. But somehow, by the grace of forces unknown to me, the result manifested. My mentor, Gerry, always told me, *"It's better to be blessed than smart."* Today I couldn't agree more. It's really a blessings to see your goals manifested. So you

 Yvan Kaprielian

might ask, "What's the point of planning then?" Just like for a diamond, planning will give you a vision of the end result and a sense of direction, and it helps you focus your energy on achieving the goal and not become sidetracked by distractions. I had the opportunity to speak to Gabriella Tolkowsky a few times, and he told me something very interesting. He said that many times he would let the diamond "do the talking". What does that mean? According to him, it was as if the diamond told him how it wanted to be cut. So interesting, that's exactly what I experienced when I graded that diamond first time without the loupe at the begining of my career, I had heard the diamond talking to me. He would have a general idea, but he would just go with the flow, getting his conscious mind out of the way, letting go of wanting to control everything and just going with the flow, going with what he saw in his mind's eye. He said the result was always astonishing. Things didn't always go as planned, but the result was always the same—a magnificent diamond.

Determining the final shape of the diamond is also directly related to the shape of the original rough.

I can you tell you that this book you're reading right now actually started off as a reference guide I created in 1991 at the beginning of my career to help me sell diamonds to my clients. My English and speaking abilities were very limited, so I developed a binder with images and diagrams and formulated various chapters from my own research and my GIA books. That was the best way for me at the time to sell diamonds. The point of origin, the rough and uncut aspect of this book is a direct reflection of my original reference guide from twenty-five years earlier. It had pictures and chapters in it and its purpose was to educate. There was no way I could have known that at the point of origin. Just like in diamonds, the finished and faceted diamond is a reflection of the original rough and uncut diamond. So you may ask, "Was I planning to write a book all along?" The answer is no. I knew what I wanted and was clear on that—to help people understand the topic of diamonds before they went ahead and spent their money on this mysterious object. But by remaining flexible and asking different questions, by changing my angle of observation, I was able to see that I could reach more people with a book and share the essence of my experiences without even being there. Hence, the reason why I wrote this book as if I'm having a conversation with you, although with less corny jokes. I'll explain in a later chapter the importance of changing your angle of observation.

Many rough diamonds out there have odd shapes. During the crystallization process, very intense temperatures and pressure will force the rough diamond to take various shapes. Distortions in the crystal structure will cause the diamond to be more difficult to plan for the cut. Various clarity characteristics will be *picked up* during their natural growth process, and small fissures may develop inside of the rough crystal, making the cutting process more challenging.

The Initial Cut

At this point the planning is complete. The diamond is mapped out, and it is brought to the cutting station. The next step is to give it the initial strike. Usually, diamonds are cleaved with a tool called the cleaver. It's a sharp-looking tool that resembles a chisel. The cutter places it right on the marked location on the rough diamond. He takes a deep breath and in an instant, without hesitation, he strikes. And *bam*, the first step is done.

As technology improved over the years, diamonds started being cut with a sawing process. In the more recent years, the use of the laser entered the industry. From this point on, there is no going back. The diamond is cleaved or cut in two parts, and the cutter must continue to the next step. You see, it's the same for our lives. Once we are done with the planning, we then must take the initial step and act. Right before the cutter hits the diamond, he makes a decision that cannot be reversed. We are just the same. We make the decision to take control of our lives, and from that point on, there is no turning back. The origin of the word *decision* comes from the mid-fifteenth century Old French and Latin root *dēcīsiō*, which literally means cutting off. So it's like having two options. You must choose one to keep and cut out. Usually in a really well-formed octahedron, and when clarity characteristics permit, both parts can be used. However, one will be significantly larger. Take a look at the next diagram.

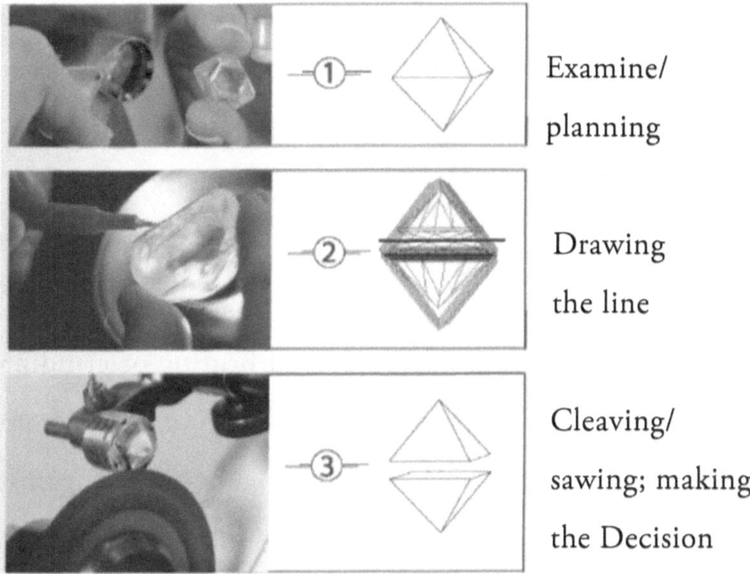

Photo courtesy of IGI (International Gemological Institute)

At some point, hopefully sooner rather than later, you must draw the line and move forward in order to live a better life. Leave no possible way to retreat. There must be only one choice at that point, and that it is to move forward. Indecision is usually worse than a wrong decision. Why? Because indecision has no end, it keeps you in limbo and stagnation and leads to massive procrastination. If you make a decision and it turns out to be a bad one, at least you'll know sooner. You'll learn from it, and your next decision will be better. The basic message is that we must make that *decision* and keep moving forward.

Bruting

Let's round things up! The process of bruting or grinding is nothing more than making your diamond round from the rough. It's placed on a lathe and engine-turned against another diamond to make one round. Only a diamond can cut another, so they are placed against each other to get the job done. Sometimes you can get both round at the same time. And that's it! That's all there is to it. Nothing more to say!

But is it really just that…?

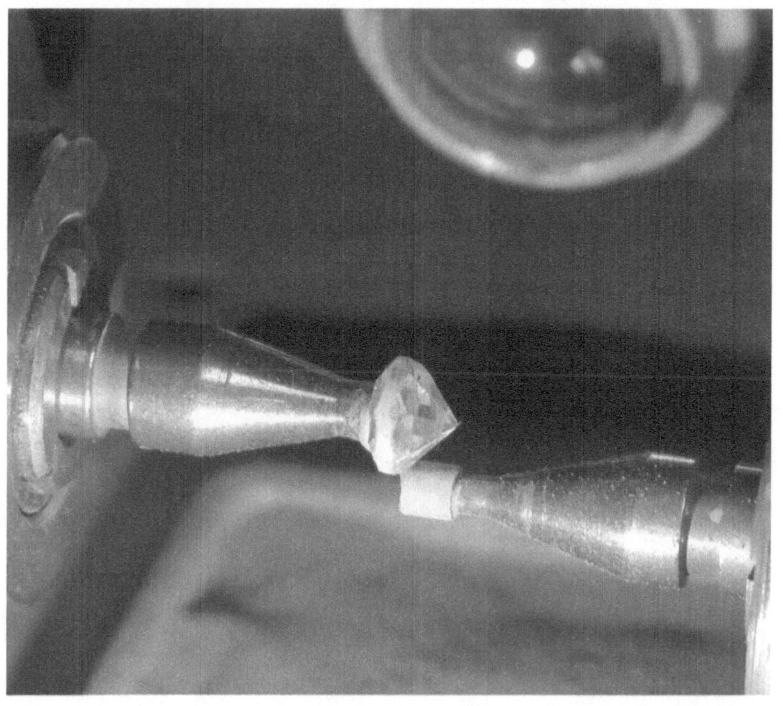

This is a very interesting turning point (no pun intended) for diamond cutting. Let's get in a time machine and travel back to the 1800s for a moment, shall we? This was a time when many scientists from around the world seemed to be in a rat race to begin harnessing the potential power of electricity. The light bulb officially came about in 1879. The invention of the electric motor took a period of about forty years from the mid-1850s to the early 1890s. Nicolas Tesla was the first to work on electric motors through a multiphase system with alternating current. He was the first to develop the basics and the first to present the principles of a multiphase induction motor. This was sometime around 1888. This invention changed the world, including the diamond industry, and many other industries. The introduction of the electric motor in the diamond industry led to the development of the old European cut. This cut was the precursor of the modern round brilliant I've explained earlier. During this period of about thirty to forty years from the 1890s to the 1930s, round diamonds were called old European. Before that period diamonds were not really round. They were mostly Cushion-shaped and mimicked the shape of the rough diamond from which they were cut, the octahedron I described in an earlier chapter, two four-sided pyramids base to base. Those were called the Old Mine cut or the Old Minor.

Let's dig a little deeper! What's even more interesting is that those old mine cuts had larger facets than the old European cut. So you might say, "What's the big deal?" Well, many people have asked me that question, at least the people who really wanted to discover the secrets and the origins of diamonds and diamond cutting. So I'm going to unveil this for you.

Around 1879 to 1880, Thomas Edison introduced for the first time a marketable incandescent light bulb that lasted six hundred hours. But before the widespread and reliable use of electric light bulbs, candles and oil lamps were still used for light. Candles give off a very soft and soothing light, and earlier light bulbs did not have the intensity of the light we know of today, so diamond cutters were limited to that type light. They also didn't fully understand the brilliance potential of a diamond. Therefore, for the lack of better lighting and understanding, facets on a diamond were cut larger to absorb and reflect more of that soft light. It wasn't until the widespread use of the electric light bulb that diamonds started being faceted with smaller facets. More concentration of brighter light led to smaller facets, more scintillation, and increased brilliance. As lighting technology improved, so did diamond cutting in parallel. Since diamonds were all about light refraction and reflection, this parallel was inevitable. When we combined this simultaneous emergence of new lighting and the use of the electric motor to make a diamond perfectly round, we were opening an entire new chapter in diamond cutting. In 1919, Marcel Tolkowsky saw that opportunity and mathematically redesigned the now well-known modern round brilliant. The focus on light return was made possible, which in turn drove a demand to refine cutting yet once again. But until then, the primary focus was on weight retention. When you brute or grind a diamond to make it round, you lose valuable carat weight and drive the profits down since diamonds are bought and sold by weight. However, this new cutting strategy gave way to improve brilliance and desirability, but it also demanded more skills and time, therefore driving prices back up again. Consumers started to look for more brilliant diamonds, so fine cutting became just as important as weight. The importance of precise facet alignment was born.

So you see, there's always a good reason for everything.

In the diamond industry, nothing is left to chance.

Most people pay little or no attention or know little to nothing about this step. However, in a few pages, we can see the major role and impact it had on the diamond industry and how we see diamonds today.

How can we parallel this to our lives? Simple! When you trace back the chronology of the evolution of your life, you will find that every little step, no matter how insignificant they may seem at that time, had a significant to drastic impact on every facets of your life—whether positive or negative. Each stepping stone has its significance and an important role to play in your life. These are just words on paper in a book, yet they could change the way you see your life and hopefully help you improve it. In the diamond industry, there's very little to practically no emphasis on this step. You'll find a few lines just like the few lines I wrote in the paragraph at the beginning of this section, but this step was the catalyst and main pivot in the diamond industry as we know it. So what are your catalysts? What are the pivots in your life? If you start digging, you'll come to realize that what seemed to be irrelevant could be a massive pivot and a catalyst that caused you to change for the better or for the worse. It all depends on which angle of observation you choose to see it.

Faceting

The next stage of cutting is called faceting. This is the step where the eight main and larger facets are cut. In this case, cutting facets is referred to as polishing facets. We don't actually *cut* facets as the diamond is too hard to cut such small surfaces. Most people think diamond facets are *chipped off* or cut off like you would cut an apple with a knife. They are not. The only way to make a facet is by polishing it or grinding it down if you prefer. The diamond is held in a tool called a dop and is applied onto a turntable disk made of fine cast iron.

Photo courtesy of GIA (Gemological Institute of America)

This disk also rotates at a very specific and steady speed. The disk has special lubricants and abrasives on it, usually a mix of special oils and very fine diamond dust. As only a diamond can cut another, only diamond dust can polish a diamond. Each master cutter has his own recipe for that mix, and none will reveal what it is. I've heard they used to use olive oil in the past, and some still do today, but that's one thing no one has shared with me yet. Another trade secret! This lubricant allows the diamond facets to be polished smoothly and without burning the surface. Have you ever sanded wood with a handheld sander? If you have, I'm sure you have noticed that if you push too hard and too long on the same spot, you may get a burn mark on the surface of the wood. Has that ever happened to you? Well, the same thing happens with a diamond on the polishing wheel. If the stone is being pushed too hard and too long, the surface being polished can burn. Then it becomes a longer process to remove the burnt part, and the facet may overextend itself and overflow onto the adjacent facets. The faceting process will end up taking more time than needed, and you may lose more diamond weight. So what's the message? When you work on polishing one of your facets, take the appropriate amount of time. You don't want to overdo it and end up making mistakes. For instance, if you are working on your financial facet and want to improve it, rushing into any type of investments will not be the smart thing to do. I am not an investment expert here, but I know enough to understand that by placing your money in stocks without doing research on the companies and the market, you can lose all the money you invested. You will then lose time rebuilding that loss, and although you might get back to your original amount of money, one thing you will never get back is time. And this extra time you'll use to rebuild your funds will also be sacrificed at the expense of another aspect of your life, an adjacent facet. I love diamonds, but time is more precious. Are you seeing the parallel? I see a lot people working nonstop and crazy long hours. All they do is work. I was one of them not too long ago. If you are constantly working and keep pushing yourself to the limits, you will eventually burn out. Granted, sometimes we have to push harder to accomplish something that may be time-sensitive, but you can't do it all the time. Once your time is spent, it's never coming back. The most precious thing in your life that you can invest is your time, so invest wisely.

Losing time is like losing diamond weight. Once it's gone, it's gone. Master cutters understand that, so if it's going to take a little longer to polish a facet on the diamond in order to get the best results for brilliance, they will take their time.

On the other hand, if the cutter doesn't apply enough pressure on the diamond the polishing wheel, absolutely nothing happens. It would be as if he's just sitting there, hoping the diamond will polish all by itself. So how does this lesson apply to our lives? If you don't apply enough force in making your dream come true, hoping and thinking positive isn't going to cut it. If you don't have enough pressure, nothing happens, and if you have too much pressure, you burn out. Look at the many facets of your life. Where have you pushed and rushed? Where have you not done enough? Does any of this sound familiar? I remember one time when I worked for a large diamond company. I really had to apply this concept. I was traveling six to seven days a week for five months straight, putting together what we called "Diamond Events" or trunk shows if you prefer. There were so many facets that had to be polished. I had to complete so many various tasks to make each show successful it made my head spin. Between making the line of designs, preparing the display elements, selecting and buying the diamonds for each design, making sure the advertising and marketing material were sent on time to the newspapers, following up on the production of the jewelry, and assessing proper quality control, there were so many things to do, so many facets to work on. And by the way, I saw each of these events as a unique diamond, each needing to be cut and faceted properly given the event location and need in order for them to be successful, to achieve maximum brilliance. I knew if I pushed too hard at the beginning, I would be burnt out halfway into the project. I also knew if I didn't push hard enough, nothing would get done. Can you imagine hoping and thinking positive about your ads to just show up in the newspaper without having supplied the printer with your materials? "I know it will be published! I know it will be published! I know it will be published!" That mantra just won't cut it. So I had to pace myself to get the job done. I am certain that some of you at one time or another have had similar experiences. Maybe you're in that moment now?!

                                                    Yvan Kaprielian

This is true in virtually every facets of our lives. Everything has to be done with the right amount of pressure and timing. In spiritual terms this is a part of the principle of moderation. GMCKS teaches this in depth. You can't do too much, but you can't do too little either. I think it is an important part of our development. For me it was a great lesson to learn, and I'm still in the process since there are so many layers of understanding. I had the tendency to be too extreme. It was either too much or nothing at all. Think about the different facets of your life. Think about your physical facets. Are you doing any kind of exercise? Is it too little or too much? Believe it or not, you can do too much exercise and exhaust yourself and eventually hurt yourself.

Think about your mental facet. Are you doing any type of studying? What are you reading? And I don't mean the newspapers or posts on Facebook, Twitter, Instagram, Pinterest, or other forms of social media. I mean books or materials that contribute to your mental and intellectual growth. I strongly believe and recommend that studying is very important for the development of our mental faculties. Studying stimulates the brain and mind and helps keep our focus on growth and not stagnation. We all need to get our mind working and learning better ways to live and not just on our personal level but as a community. Proper mental activity is the key in keeping good mental health. You will be making new neural connections or neural pathways, which help in keeping your brain active so that you don't rely on habit mode and coast on an autopilot that eventually will loop back to stagnation. I have seen older folks working and constantly learning new things about their business and always keeping their minds occupied on positive things. They are really sharp, not just mentally but physically as well.

Do you have a balanced diet? In my opinion, this is one of the most important facet of our lives. I believe it is absolutely crucial to have a proper diet. There was a time in my life when I had a very bad diet. I wanted to be vegetarian, so I stopped eating meats. I wanted to have a healthier diet, but I didn't get proper guidance. I started gaining weight because I turned toward breads and cheeses and high-fat and high-sugar foods. I used to be a major sugar addict. You see, my diet was not balanced. Diet alone can be paralleled to a diamond. There are so many facets to consider, and they all need to be in balance.

                                        Yvan Kaprielian

And again, you must have great balance for great brilliance. I won't go into nutrition details in this book. I still have a lot to learn myself, but maybe in a future publication we could spend some time together and dive deeper into it. Our body is intimately connected to our emotions. If you don't feel good inside, how do you expect to manifest greatness in your life outside? If you always feel heavy, feel sick, or sluggish and tired, how do you expect your dreams to blossom into the magnificence they deserve? This is critical. You must take care of your body.

The body and the mind are subtle

instruments of the Soul.

~ Grand Master Choa Kok Sui ~

Both mind and body need to function harmoniously. GMCKS developed Pranic Healing for the people on the spiritual path to heal themselves and others in order to focus on their spiritual development. How is your spiritual facet?

Spirituality is also a key facet to your brilliance. Spirituality has been very important in my life. I've had many teachers in my life. I've had the opportunity to learn many lessons directly from my teacher, Grand Master Choa Kok Sui, who taught me everything I know about the essence of my being, who is the I AM inside. While learning directly from him, I found my answers, and that was when my quest for meaning started. Many of my reference in this book come directly from his teachings. We are beings of light. Our souls are made of light. And our physical bodies and their many aspects are just like diamonds. This is the main reason for this book. Look at yourself as a spiritual being of light having a human experience. Many great teachers have said that. In deeper spiritual and esoteric teachings, the Creator is described as the ultimate and infinite source of Light. We should have balance in every facet of our life in order to receive the Light and shine back as much of it as we can, just like a diamond. This Light should be reflected back out to the ones that are seeing you. It means everyone around you. How do you feel when you see a diamond that has so much life and brilliance? Don't you instantly feel joy and happiness? Your face changes. You start to smile, and your eyes open up really wide, trying to absorb as much light as this diamond is reflecting. I've been witnessing that for the past twenty-five years. Don't you think we would be just like a diamond if all facets of our lives were in harmony with one another? A diamond is all about reflecting that light that is given to it. It doesn't hold anything back. A diamond is all about sharing the light. The more light you give it, the more it's going to shine. A diamond does not discriminate any viewer. It will shine no matter what anyone says, thinks, or feels. I have seen diamonds that were so well balanced and cut that they were blinding under intense light. I put one under a laser pointer, and I was amazed by the reflection patterns I saw. I was amazed that the intensity of the laser was not only maintained but also amplified and multiplied by the amount of facets it reflected from. By the way, don't try this at home unless you are super careful. The reflections of the laser will be just as bright as if you pointed the laser directly in your eyes. Be careful. Protect your eyes, or don't do it at all! Trust me on this one.

I realized that as human beings, we must balance out all of our facets and be just like a diamond. Diamonds have the ability to split that light, distribute it evenly, and reflect it back with incredible brilliance and without losing the original intensity. Even in a dark place, a diamond will absorb the little diffused light there is, amplify it through the many facets, and reflect it back with an amazing and dazzling dance of reflections. It's so important that we understand that our life is just waiting to get cut and recut until we have harmony. There are many diamonds out there that are not perfectly balanced, and that's fine. Just understand that no matter how they are cut, they reflect light. How do you want to reflect the light that is given to you?

Too Shallow or Too Deep?

I must also say that sometimes diamonds won't reflect light very well because they are too shallow. In the diamond industry, they are called *fisheye*. The crown, which is the part above the girdle, may be too flat, or the pavilion, the part below the girdle, isn't deep enough. So a lot of the light is lost because it goes right through it and never gets a chance to be reflected back out.

Where's the connection? Think about it. Have you ever heard of the term *shallow* to describe a person? Unfortunately, as terrible as it sounds, there are individuals who are labeled as shallow people and seem to have no balance in their lives. Being shallowis not a very good thing, but it can be changed with a few simple steps. It's called recutting and realigning the facets.

There are also diamonds that are the opposite. The crown may be too high, or the pavilion may be too deep. In the diamond industry, they are called *nail-head*. They look dark in the center. It's the same thing with people. These individuals go into things too deeply and don't allow enough the light to be reflected. Take a look at the diagram.

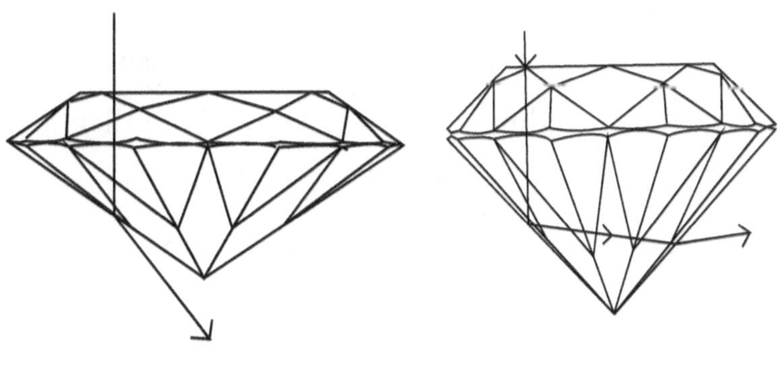

Too shallow   *Too deep*

It shows you the differences between too shallow and too deep.

The next diagram shows what a well-cut diamond should look like.

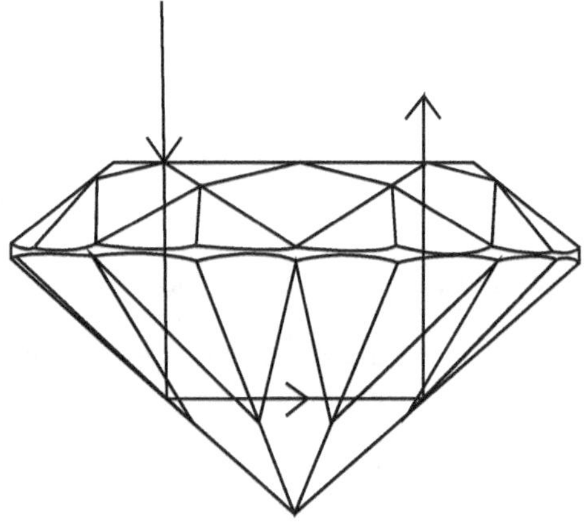

Let me take you a step further and really get to the core of the message. This next diagram is really important because it connects everything there is to know about diamonds and their message. It shows the critical angle. Once you understand what really happens to the light inside the diamond, you will understand the importance of facet angles and alignment.

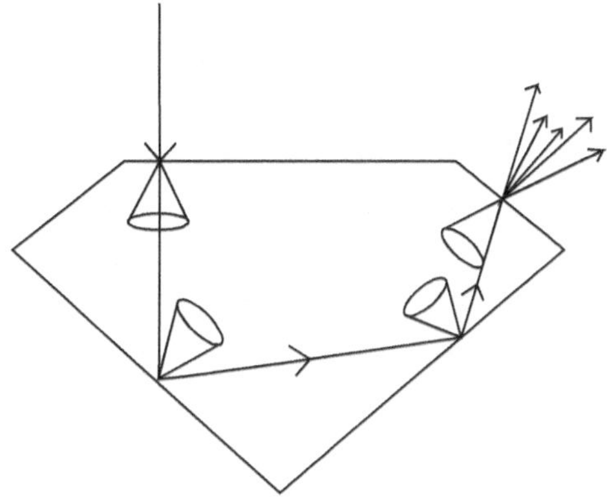

The straight line represents the light. Notice also the cone-shaped figures. Notice how the light enters the diamond and goes through the first cone. Then as it continues to travel, it stays outside the second and third cone, but when it reaches the fourth cone and goes right into it, the light exits the diamond. In optics this cone is called the critical angle. Inside the diamond the light has to stay outside the critical angle, but in order for the light to come back out and be reflected toward the observer, it must pass through the critical angle. This means that this angle represents a certain degree of internal discipline, so to speak, in order to maintain proper brilliance. Light can enter the diamond only through that cone within that angle and can only exit through that cone within that angle. In our lives we must be just the same. Our internal discipline must be such that we keep ourselves focused on making sure that we have our facets in balance. The second and third cones are what I call *traps*. They become the degree of intolerance. If the light falls in that trap, it's lost, and maximum brilliance cannot be achieved. Let me put it in another way. Think of those days when you decided to get yourself on a specific diet or made a specific resolution to improve yourself in a certain way. At the beginning you followed every step carefully, making sure you do everything right. You felt really good about yourself and perhaps even started seeing results. Then after a certain period of time, you start deviating from that path. It starts to feel as if it's getting harder to achieve results. Then shortly after that, you find yourself really off course. And when someone who knows about your resolution or goal asks you how you are doing, what's the usual answer you give? Or if you have asked other people that question, how do they respond? The most common answer is "I fell off the wagon" or "I fell off track." If only I had written down how many times I fell off the wagon or fell off track before completing my book, it would most likely fill more pages than the book itself. Seriously, if you trace the chain of events back in your mind and find the point where you fell

                                                  Yvan Kaprielian

off, which should not be too hard of a task if you're honest with yourself, you'll know the exact point of entry into the critical angle, the trap. That's the point of origin when you started veering off and losing light, or experiencing light leakage as it is called in the diamond industry.

This can really help you identify the trigger that sets you off course. You can then in turn polish that facet and redirect the light in the desired direction. By the way, this is exactly one of the main reasons why New Year's resolutions hardly ever work.

Yes, these cones look small, but don't forget everything inside the diamond is in multi-dimension perspective, and we live in a multi-dimensional world. Believe me, a little difference in angles and facet alignment does make it easy to fall in these traps. The diagram shows only one ray of light and only four cones. Inside that diamond there is an infinite amount of rays, but there is also an infinite amount of cones or traps. It's all in the balance, you can't have more of one or the other. This is another reason why we should maintain a balanced life. Taking things too extremes in your life is like allowing the light to fall inside those cones. You will lose light, and you will lose brilliance. We have control over our facets just like the diamond cutter has control of the final look of the diamond. It's all in our hands. I know this sounds complicated and technical, but with a little thought, you should see it clearly. We could explore this section in greater depth, but for the initial purpose of this book, I wanted to keep it light. No pun intended!

Chapter IV
The Setting

Resetting your stone by taking the diamond out of the old ring mounting is like removing yourself from the claws of your past that hold you back—claws that prevent you from growing, improving, and moving forward in your life to better, newer, and more beautiful things. Claws are like patterns, habits, and belief systems that do nothing more than hold you back. Even though they are old and worn out and barely serve their purpose, they still hold you back. But they are fragile and can break very easily when pulled in the opposite direction. When they do break, the diamond comes out, and it's lost forever. You look down at your hand, and all you see in an empty space in the middle of your ring in between these old worn-out prongs. When and where did you lose that diamond and how it came out is always the big mystery. You end up searching, backtracking in your mind when was the last time you looked at your ring, trying to retrace everywhere you were up until the painful moment you realized it was gone … forever.

Our life is just the same. Old belief systems, patterns, and habits tend to let us down when we least expect it. When and where did we lose ourselves is always the big mystery. Some of us don't even realize there's something old and obsolete that needs major improvement. Then one day someone with knowledge and skills comes along to show us that these prongs are old. I saw this time and time again when I gave recommendations to my clients to get new settings before they lost their stones, and they didn't listen. They would come back a few months later with tears in their eyes. It would break my heart to see these people with so much emotional pain. They had attached so many emotions to that ring, to that diamond. What can we do about it?

Some of us recognize that something is wrong, that the ring is in bad shape, that the prongs are worn out and barely holding. Those old beliefs systems, patterns, and habits are barely serving their purpose. They are old and worn-out, but again, we don't make a change.

Some of us recognize that something needs improvement, and we look for a quick fix. In jewelry terms, that is called *retipping* your prongs. Basically, it's adding soldering metal on top of these old prongs. That's nice, but it never lasts very long because it's just on the surface. In our society that's something often refer to as a "quick-fix". I'm not going to list all the different kinds of "quick-fixes", I'm certain you can imagine those on your own. But you know, these solutions are only treating the symptoms on the surface and not going to the root. It's a quick-fix and doesn't cost that much, although it does depends on the "fixes" some people would actually choose. It's a repair, and repairing implies taking something old and trying to make it work for the time being. It implies that something new will eventually need to take its place, or there will be negative consequences without a doubt.

Then you have some of us who recognize that something is old and worn-out and decide to actually do something substantial about it. That's when real change takes place. They seek expert advice and look around to see what's available, what's new, and how to make those changes and improvements. For diamonds there are preexisting settings that are ready to go. There are pre-made mountings that could work great for your diamond. Some of us prefer going the custom route, and that's perfectly fine too. They are experts that will love to help you design your perfect setting. So you see, just like a diamond can be reset into a preset setting or a custom design, you can do the same for your life. All you have to do is decide what kind setting you want to be in. There's that word again—decision! If you don't like your setting or your environment, then get out there and customize one. Design it the way you want it to be for your life. Some experts would love to help you create just what you really want. But you must make a DECISION.

So you might ask, "Where do I start? How do I know if I need a new setting? What kind of setting do I want?" Well, these are great questions. There's a series of important steps to take, and in the next chapter we're going to explore how it's done in the jewelry business and then how it relates to our lives.

There are many things to consider when starting on a new path. In Pranic Healing and Arhatic Yoga, GMCKS teaches in detail about the spiritual approach to making these changes by using energy and advanced meditations to disintegrate those old patterns and habits and create new ones. You will learn how the old patterns are affecting your life, and you will learn how to minimize the negative and how to amplify the positive. His teachings are very simple but very powerful. By understanding how energy works, you will have a deeper understanding of the bad habits and thereby eliminate them and replace them with better ones. Keep in mind, these prongs, these patterns habits and beliefs system are important. They give us structure and stability, regardless of their nature. If they are bad, they'll give you stability and structure in the bad. If they are good they will give you stability and structure in that same respect. Be wise about your observation.

NOTES

Chapter V
The Process

They are eight steps to take in order to achieve your goal.

Step 1: Diagnostics

Take a good look at your ring, your setting, and your diamond. With a little common sense, you'll notice if the prongs and the entire setting are old and worn-out. Get closer to it and touch the top with your finger. Does it feel sharp? Is it catchy? Is there anything caught between the diamond and the prongs? One or more of these tests will be indicators. Also, figure out how many years you have had it. How often do you wear it? Is it yellow gold, white gold, or platinum? Why is it important to know the nature of the metal? Platinum will outlast gold because of its overall durability and its density. As a side note, let's get a little technical and veer off topic for a little if you don't mind, there are important points we need to discuss. You see, gold and platinum are very soft metals at their pure state when found in nature. When you buy gold jewelry in the United States, it's mostly 14 karat (kt) and 18 karat for higher priced items or imported jewelry. 14kt is 58.5% pure gold and 41.5% an alloy mixture. These alloy metals are much less expensive and harder metals. Copper is very common and almost always used as an alloy ingredient. It's a little harder and much cheaper in comparison to gold. It hardens the gold when mixed, rendering it more wearable and therefore increasing the jewelry's life span. This is particularly true for rings and bracelets as they can endure much more *abuse* than earrings or necklaces. The 18kt gold is 75% pure and 25% an alloy mixture. The same applies here; however, the alloy content is decreased, and the softer nature of the gold is dominant. It is well known that 18kt is softer than 14kt. This is the reason why. It also costs more simply because of the higher gold content. One difference within the gold jewelry family is white and yellow colors. You might have heard that white gold is harder than yellow. That's true. The gold content in white gold remains the same for 14kt or 18kt as it is in yellow gold. It's the nature of the alloys that changes. It's also well known that white gold is often mixed with nickel in many main stream jewelry. People who have nickel allergies will not buy white gold for that reason. However, there are two reasons why nickel is used as an allow. First, it renders gold closer to a white look and makes it hard. Second, it's very cheap. I'll tell you from experience that I never really liked working with white gold. It's hard and brittle. When setting diamonds in prongs, you have to do the job right on the first try. If the stone is not sitting right and needs to be taken out to re-cut the prongs, pushing the metal back and forth more than twice will weaken the prongs and leave it prone to cracking and breaking. It may not crack right there and then, but sometimes it does. Either way, working with it will still weaken the prongs. An easy-to-understand analogy would be the paper clip example. Have you ever bent a paperclip back and forth a few times? If so, you know that the metal just cracks in half after a few times. This is what happens to prongs when manipulated too much. Perhaps this is why sometimes white gold prongs on finished jewelry seem be missing after a few months of wearing. By nature of the mix, if 58.5% (14kt) or even more so 75% (18kt) is yellow, the end result will still have a yellow look to it. It will still look as an off-white color with a yellow undertone. So by industry accepted standards, white gold is plated with rhodium. Rhodium is part of the platinum family and used only as a plating agent. It gives the surface of white gold a super bright, chrome-like finish. I've had people come to me and ask if the rings they bought during their vacations were made of real gold or if they got ripped off. The bottom of the ring was starting to look yellow, and they thought they had been taken for a ride. After about six months to a year of wear, your ring or bracelet may start looking yellow in some places. That's because that rhodium plating is starting to wear off and the true color of the white gold is being revealed—that is, assuming it is gold to start with. Can it be re-plated? Yes, however to do the job right, the jewelry will need to be re-polished fully in order to apply the rhodium properly and achieve a longer lasting finish. Polishing implies removing metal at a micron level and therefore contributing to the wear of the jewelry. If you do this two or three times in a ten-year period, I can promise you it will severely affect the durability of the piece in question. On less expensive jewelry or costume jewelry, the same principle applies. The only difference is that the rhodium is diluted with nickel, or it's just nickel altogether. It's a big allergy problem for sensitive people! Clean rhodium by itself is hypoallergenic. It is used to plate yellow gold, including 10kt, 14kt, and 18kt, and it's used for people who have allergies to other gold alloys. It's very often used for earring posts to solve the problem of skin irritation on the earlobe and sometimes inside rings for finger irritation. And even more so, sometimes the posts are just replaced with platinum posts, which is also hypoallergenic.

This leads us to discuss platinum. How come when we see our grandma's engagement and wedding rings they seem to still hold up well? When you look inside the rings, if a sizing process hasn't removed it, you might see a stamping inside and maybe a wedding date engraved. Many times the stamps are 90% Plat and 10% Irid. *Irid* stands for iridium, a metal that is part of the platinum family along with ruthenium, palladium, and rhodium. In newer platinum rings, you will see a "Plat 950" stamping or "PT950." This means the mix is different. It's 95% platinum and 5% alloy. In the past people used to alloy platinum with iridium. In the more recent years, platinum is also often alloyed with ruthenium. The main reason for these mixes, just like with gold, is to make the metal a little harder. Platinum is also heavier than gold because of its high density. It is on average about 47% heavier than 14kt and 18kt. It also melts at a much higher temperature than gold. Gold melting point starts at 1,950°F (1,070°C), while Platinum will start at 3,215°F (1,768°C). It's almost double! That makes a gigantic difference when it comes to working with the metals. Tools are different. The level of skill is different, and the time required in creating jewelry will also vary dramatically. In my experience most jewelers I've known will spend on average about three times as many hours in working on platinum than working on gold to do the job properly. Combine that extra work time together with higher precious metal content—95% pure vs 58.5% for 14kt gold for example—not to mention more expensive alloys, it makes sense why platinum jewelry is priced higher than gold jewelry. But one thing remains certain, the metal is as white as it gets. And it doesn't require any sort of plating. However, expect your ring to dull out over the years. When platinum starts scratching, unlike gold, it doesn't retain its luster. And as I mentioned earlier it will outlast gold by at least 3 times. I'll give you my analogy, and if you're a chocolate lover like me, you'll understand this in a heartbeat. Picture yourself taking a bar of chocolate out of the fridge and scraping it with a knife. What happens to the chocolate? As you're scraping and scratching it, you'll see that it chips off in shredding.

You're losing chocolate! Oh no! This is what happens to gold when you wear it. Microscopic pieces of gold will chip off. But the gold retains its luster. Now picture another bar of chocolate, but this time it's at room temperature in the summer, assuming it's not completely melted. Take the knife to it now. What happens? The chocolate doesn't chip off, and there is no shredding. It just moves over. This is what happens to platinum during normal wear. So in essence, you're not losing any metal, or you're losing a very minimal amount in comparison to gold. Therefore, your platinum ring will last longer than a gold ring. But in the case of platinum, it doesn't retain its new-state luster. That's the nature of platinum, you can't go around it.

There's something in this gold-platinum differences that's very much misunderstood and misrepresented, and I will explain this to you in the simplest way I can. Many jewelers often say that platinum is stronger than gold. It's true, but stronger in what sense is the big question. Earlier I have described to you the difference in resistance to scratching. Platinum will outlast gold under the same scratching conditions. However, pressure is different than scratching. Gold will endure higher pressures than platinum and will not bend as easily. So if you take two identical rings, say two millimeters thick for example, one in gold and one in platinum. When you apply the same pressure in the same manner, the platinum ring will bend quicker than the gold. I've seen this many times with wedding bands and engagement rings. This is where the confusion is. Clients would come back with their platinum rings bent out of shape and say;

"I thought this wouldn't happen with platinum because it's supposed to be stronger!"

Yes, more resilient to scratching but not to pressure. So don't do pull-ups or carry heavy bags with your ring on. I guarantee you that it will bend out of shape, even thick men's wedding bands. Perhaps it won't distort as easily as a two-millimeter band, but it will bend. I hope this is clear enough of an explanation.

Today some casting companies like to mix their 18kt white gold with palladium. Palladium is much more expensive than nickel and other alloys, but it's also more malleable. It's very white and won't require additional alloy metals or rhodium plating. I've worked with 18kt/ palladium mix, and I love it. Great alternative!

Now, after our short excursion in the vast world of precious metals, let's coming back to the first step. The diagnostic should be complete. If you're not sure, that's fine. Seek advice. I highly recommend it. Sometimes from our point of view with our own setting, it's hard to see what needs to be done. An expert could tell you but so could a good friend who can see you from a different perspective.

Step 2: Inventory

This step is two fold. First, you'll need to take an inventory and find out exactly where you are. With your ring you'll have to take inventory of your stones. Is there just one diamond, or is there a multitude of them? Are there any other stones besides diamonds? If you're using a GPS to look for a specific restaurant your friend recommended, the device will have to determine your current standing location in order to give you directions to that place. You need to know where point A is in order to get to point B. That's your personal inventory. You need to know where you're standing and what you have to work with. If there are more than one stone, how many of the stones would you like to use? If there's only one at the start, do you want to add more? Second, this step will also help you monitor your progress once you start moving forward. Knowing your starting point will help reinforce the fact that you're making the right choices, assuming of course that you are moving in that desired direction.

Step 3: Direction

You need a point of direction. You need to know what point B is. This can be a bit tricky. Where do you want to be? What's your ideal setting? You will need to figure out what you want. You have to find a purpose, or else you won't get anywhere. Imagine you're in the middle of Manhattan calling for a cab. Once you get in, the driver will say, *"Where to?"* What do you think will happened if you say, *"Heh, just drive…"* Can you guess where you'll end up? Can you guess how long you'll stay in that cab? Can you guest how much the fare will be?

Step 4: Evaluate

Evaluating how much work needs to be done before we start moving forward.

Talk to experts about your ideas and goals. There are people out there who specialize in these fields. Expert jewelers can help you save time in your research. Even with a short consultation, they can help you save a lot of time and frustration. The same is true with your life. There are experts out there who can help you. Although some people may call themselves experts, but they may not really produce measurable results. Research diligently and intelligently. Talk to true friends and family. They might be able to point out certain things that you may not see on your own or things you won't admit to yourself unless someone you trust points them out. Be careful though! The people closest to us aren't always pointing out what's best for us. They don't do this in malicious way, I doubt that. It's just hard to put ourselves in other people's shoes and see the world the way they do, even if sometimes they are close to us. Because they are close to you and care for you, they may not want to risk hurting you by saying things you don't necessarily want to hear. So take everything with a grain of salt, and evaluate everything for yourself. This is a key principle GMCKS teaches. Don't take anything at face value. Evaluate for yourself before accepting anything as truth because someone said it was the truth.

Step 5: DECIDE!

Do not take this step lightly. This is the most important step. Yes, you've heard this from me over and over again, but that's because it's very important. You can spend years building a spacecraft, but if you never fire it off into space to serve its purpose, it's totally useless. In my experience, this is when things happen. You'll have to come to the inevitable conclusion that your setting needs a change, and in turn, you'll need to make a definite decision. If you don't make a definitive decision, nothing will happen. I should say nothing significant and positive will happen to help you move forward. You might end up losing your diamond down the road. It may not be right away; however, it will eventually fall out, and you'll lose it. You can lose yourself in a lifestyle you don't like, and years can go by without you doing anything about it. This is called procrastination, the ninja habit that sneaks up on you. We've talked about this in a previous chapter. You don't want to be in this position.

What is also true is that sometimes some of us don't want to admit that a change is needed, perhaps because we are too comfortable in our current setting or perhaps even too lazy to make the necessary changes. Perhaps we think it's too hard and complicated and may take too long. Maybe we don't have the necessary funds to create a new setting, or perhaps we are in a state of denial. This is why you've created a personal inventory so you'll know where to start. But you'll need to be super honest with yourself and admit that a change is needed. And yes, this may not come as easy as you think. It's like putting yourself in front of a mirror and saying the stuff you don't want to hear about yourself. It's not easy, but it's a necessary and important step to take. Just do it! The alternative of not going through it is much more costly and much more painful in the long run.

Step 6: Taking the Stone Out

This is an interesting part of the process. Technically, we are supposed to clean the ring thoroughly before removing the diamond from the setting. It's just easier to clean the diamond because it's still mounted. However, there's always a surprise when you take it out. Under the prongs, years of accumulations of dirt isn't always easily removed by ultrasonic cleaners and steamers alone. Sometimes you must take more drastic measures. Special liquids and boiling solutions are used in order to clean the diamond properly of all old stuff. The diamond needs to undergo a cleansing phase. In our lives we need to do the same. My teacher made it clear that this was one of the pillars of proper spiritual development. This is called self-purification. We need to purify ourselves in order to move forward properly and easily. Old "stuff" left over from previous prongs and those old beliefs systems that no longer serve us need to go. If anything in the world is clean, it's more difficult to dirty it than if it's already dirty to start with. Dirt will have nothing to hold to and may not stick as easily on a clean slate. So you might say; *"That's nice, but didn't you mention earlier that diamonds always get dirty no matter what and there's no way around it?"* Yes, I did say that. We are just like diamonds. You get dirty regularly in physical, emotional, and mental ways. It doesn't matter who you are or where you live, you will need to regularly cleanse the many aspects of your being. The diamond will be much easier to clean if you clean it regularly after that initial and throughout cleansing process. It's like a dirty stove. If you don't clean it after each use and wait a few months, which is easier to clean? Yeah, that's gross but you get the point. Furthermore, you'll realize that self-purification is also an ongoing process. As you rid yourself of old stuff, new layers of "stuff" will be revealed to you. That's also something you can't go around, and yes, you'll have to do this until your last breath. At one point in time, this old dirty stuff will have to be cleansed from your system, or it will create obstacles and prevent you from moving forward and progressing in your development. The sooner you do this, the better. That's another parallel we have with diamonds. In Pranic Healing and Arhatic Yoga this is thoroughly explained how not purifying yourself can have a negative physical and psychological impact on your well-being.

 Yvan Kaprielian

Step 7: Examine the Diamond

Now is a good time to re-polish, re-cut and balance the facets to improve brilliance. When it comes to diamonds, we'll need magnification. A 10x power jewelers loupe is used for this step. Take a close look at the diamond. Does it have any chips, nicks, or abrasions? If yes, how can it be fixed? You can refer to this process as a makeover. What can you do to improve yourself? I'm not suggesting liposuction or plastic surgery here. But perhaps you can change your diet or hairstyle, sign up at a gym, take yoga classes, taker higher courses in Arhatic Yoga and Pranic Healing, learn to meditate, take classes to earn a higher degree in your current line of work or even in a totally different industry. There's always room for improvement.

Step 8: Set the Diamond

This is the fun part. Setting the diamond in the setting is really exciting. This is the culmination of all your efforts, and finally, you can start seeing results. You can now cut the new prongs and shape them the way you want. You've put in place a plan with new belief systems, created a new environment, and made physical changes. Now you're ready to move forward. Everybody's intention is to grow and be better and have more things and make more money. Everyone is eager to change their circumstances but how many are willing to change themselves in order to make that happen? That's an interesting question. I have notice that a lot of people like to talk about growing but don't take much action to move toward it. So I ask you;

"What are you willing to do to achieve your goals?"

The difference between a stumbling block and a stepping-stone is how high you are willing to raise your foot.

~ Benny Lewis ~

NOTES

Chapter VI
Transformation

In the past years, I've had the opportunity to work for a jewelry designer while I resided in Scottsdale, Arizona. During my employment there, I worked with clients who were interested in remounting their old diamond rings into a more contemporary design. This company has the unique ability to design and create amazing styles to enhance the beauty of people's jewelry. We served many clients in our community, but we also did a lot of business out of state as well. One major advantage we had was the fact that we had an entire design studio and manufacturing facility right on the premises. There was a very large showroom in the front, and the workshop was in the back. The two rooms were separated by a tall and long glass window. This allowed clients to see the entire facility and appreciate the manufacturing process. There were people from all over the United States who came to visit us all year round because they had heard of us or seen our ads in some of the most prestigious national magazines. Over the years the company became very popular, and we were far ahead of the other jewelers on the local and national level. I've had countless clients who were thrilled and proud to own one of these designs. I also had clients who came in and told me they could not stand their old jewelry because some of the pieces had been bought in regular jewelry stores. I call them "assembly line" jewelry. It's true! They are mass-produced in very large quantity and distributed across the nation, and you see them everywhere. I remember two clients in particular I met during one of our company events in October 2006. These two wonderful ladies came in to have some fun that night. I spent most of the evening with them, and they each ended up buying some beautiful designs that looked great on them. They also mentioned to me that they had a ton of jewelry at home they were not wearing anymore. They just weren't happy with the pieces because the designs were too traditional or worn-out. We set up a time for a visit so I could take a look at what they had. They had so much jewelry! One of them—I'll call her J for the sake of protecting her identity—brought me twelve rings and two pendants. The other lady—let's call her S—had two rings with big diamonds. J had a four-carat round brilliant diamond with baguettes on the side mounted on platinum. There were some rubies on some other rings, and a bunch of other rings were filled with all shapes and sizes of diamonds. S had one ring mounted in the traditional three-stone setting, also known as the "Past, Present, and Future" ring. All three stones were Emerald cut. The center one was three carats, and the two side ones were a little more than a carat each. I examined one ring a time, and after a short while, I looked at them and said;

"Ladies, are you ready for transformation?" They answered; *"What do you mean?"*

"Do you think you have nice jewelry here? Do you think you have nice diamonds?" I replied.

They both said;

"Yes, I think I do. They were expensive! But I'm not really sure!"

                                                    Yvan Kaprielian

J said;

"We've been married for more than forty years now. My husband got me this ring for our 25th anniversary. When we got married, we did not have that kind of money, so I had a little diamond, and on our 25th he surprised me with this four-carat ring. It means a lot to me."

S said;

"Yvan, I have not worn mine in a while. I just don't like the way it looks anymore. It's too plain, and it does nothing for me. I know you just cleaned it, and the diamonds look nice and all. But it still doesn't do much for me. And besides, it was given to me by my ex-husband!"

Maybe that was the real reason she didn't like it anymore, but I didn't say anything. As I mentioned previously, diamonds are the most emotionally charged product a person can give another, and I think this is the proof.

After figuring out what we had to work with and recording that on paper, we started designing. In the beginning we did not really know what direction to go in. There were so many possibilities, so many designs. By looking at many design options and by questioning what we liked and didn't like, we narrowed it down to just a few great designs.

The next step was to draw a final rendering and get it approved by the ladies. Usually, most people can visualize what the ring would look like by looking at a 3-D drawing. Of course, just like looking at the blueprint of a house, it can be a little challenging to see the depths and colors very well, but this is where faith and trust in the creator comes into play. Sometimes for clients who really had a hard time seeing the end result, I would simply say to just leave it to the masters and trust that the new ring will come out perfect. And I must say that 99% of the time, they were totally satisfied. For the other 1%, a minor adjustment would suffice. Many times the completed design ended up being better than expected. By the way at that time, CAD and 3D computer rendering was not as widespread as it is today, so all drawings were done by hand, black on white.

So where am I going with this? How does this relate to our lives? Well, I would say once again it's fairly simple. Diamonds are mounted in settings. Sometimes the setting is old and worn-out or just simply doesn't allow people to see the beauty of the diamond. Too often I have seen diamonds that are literally buried in the settings and that look like they are sunk into the metal and stuck there forever. Our lives are the same way. Too often I see people, including me, leading lives that don't allow their true beauty to come out. When I was younger and still living with my parents, I thought I was in the right setting. I thought I was shining to my full potential—that is, until I **decided** to reset myself into a new setting. So I did exactly what I did with all my clients when they came in to reset their diamonds. I looked at what I had to work with, the diagnostic process as described earlier. I asked myself;

"What are my strengths, my assets, my attributes, my strong points, my qualities, and also my weaknesses? Is my current setting serving me well, and is it serving my purpose?

Then I had to figure out what was important to me. And following closely, I had to **decide** what I wanted my new setting to look like. I started looking at my life as a diamond, trying to balance out all my facets, all aspects of my life. I started recutting my diamond and found out that although my diamond, my life, had tremendous potential for total balance and harmony, the setting was also an important part. The setting is what will give it a structure for this brilliance to shine and to be seen. I've done this many times over in my life. These two ladies' diamonds were beautiful. I recognized them the moment I saw them, but they were in the wrong setting. Those settings didn't allow the stones to sparkle. That's where the transformation process begins. Once you figure out what is most important, the next step is to start designing. Take out a sheet of paper and literally design what you want your life to look like. What setting would best describe you? I always asked my clients;

"What kind of person are you? Are you conservative, or do you like to be the center of attention? Do you like to be noticed, or are you more reserved? Are you a contemporary or more of a classic person?"

This design doesn't necessarily have to represent only one facet of your life. You could apply this analogy to your work and/or your environment and surroundings. You could be a very talented person, but if you are working for the wrong company, how do you expect to use your talents and skills to their full potential? How do you expect to display your full brilliance?

NOTES

Chapter VII

The Light

Pillar of Light

Purification and receptivity are the keys.

Let's dive into the essence of the spirit. When practicing Twin Hearts meditation, you increase the entry point of the Pillar of Light. Your ability to receive and reflect Light depends on your degree of purity, which is also connected to your degree of receptivity.

What is the Light? There are many ways to describe the Light. Many cultures and traditions around the world have their own way of describing the Light, but they are all pointing at the same thing. In many spiritual and religious books, there are similar stories with different words describing and pointing at the same thing.

We are all conduits of Light, Divine Love, and pure consciousness. The Light is pure, plainly and simply put. Our goal is to purify ourselves and strive to receive the Light and reflect it back as unaltered as possible. Eventually, we will succeed, but when? In this lifetime? I don't know. I'm in no position to judge or tell you, and I don't think anyone can answer that question. In the grand scheme of things, it doesn't really matter because that's not the point. We are not in a race to enlightenment. We must continue to purify ourselves and work our way toward that ultimate achievement. If you look at it as my diamond analogy, we'll have to take this to the atomic level.

What is a diamond made of? It's pure carbon atoms, the letter "C" on the periodic table of elements. Simple, isn't it? It's pure carbon, and the key word is pure. Yes, there are trace elements present, but the greater majority of gem quality diamonds used in the jewelry industry are 99.9998% pure. There are diamonds out there totally free from any trace elements and inclusions, 100% pure carbon. GIA classifies them as Type-IIa diamonds. They are extremely rare and crazy expensive. I'm so lucky, I've come across quite a few in my career and I've gotten the opportunity to examine them with my loupe. Wow! They are magnificent. Although you can't see the difference from a D FL, the cutter will take extra time to make sure it is perfect. The most magnificent I ever got to see and work with, meaning that I actually presented this diamond to potential buyers, was the Archduke Joseph .

It is an Antique Cushion FL (flawless) D color Type-IIa weighing 76.02ct mounted on a necklace. One of my previous employers owned it. To give you a perspective on price, it sold in November 2012 in Geneva at a Christi's auction for $21.5 million.

Some colleagues of mine have asked why I spent so much time looking at those types of diamonds with the loupe. They are flawless. There's nothing to see!! That's funny, but that's exactly the point. They are perfectly flawless and totally colorless! This is called staring into nothingness. I examine how they are faceted, which in this case is a critical and a very important aspect not to miss. If you want to understand a diamond, you have to understand how it is cut and faceted.

Our internal characteristics are like inclusions in the diamond. In the Diamond industry, these inclusions or

                                   Yvan Kaprielian

clarity characteristics are graded using a specific chart. Here is a snapshot:

- FL - Flawless
- IF - Internally Flawless.
- VVS1 - VVS2 - Very, Very Slightly included.
- VS1 - VS2 - Very Slightly included.
- SI1 - SI2 - Slightly included.
- I1 - I2 - I3 - Imperfect.

Which one are you? Of course, the idea here is not to make you feel bad. As much as 99.9% of diamonds recovered from mines have trace elements and inclusions to one degree or another. As matter of fact, only approximately 25% of diamonds found are suitable for jewelry. The rest are used for various industrial purposes, as they are too heavily included. The flawless diamonds are very rare. These inclusions have a certain degree of influence on the light being absorbed and reflected back out.

Want to know a little more? Let's take a very brief and simplified crash course on chemistry and spectroscopy! There are many types of trace elements and impurities found in diamonds, and one well known and most widely found in diamonds is nitrogen. The diamonds with zero traces of nitrogen fall in that Type-IIa category described earlier, and there are extremely rare. Nitrogen is what gives the diamond a yellow color. Well, it doesn't actually color the diamond like you would dye your Easter eggs. To put it in simple terms, nitrogen atoms attached themselves to the carbon atoms of the diamond, and when light passes through the diamond, a portion of the spectrum of the light is absorbed and filtered by the nitrogen, thus giving the diamond a yellowish color. Depending on the degree of nitrogen present, the spectroscopic properties of the diamond will change and will display varying degree of yellow color intensity. The same is true for other colors. The presence of boron will be seen as blue. None harmful radiation will be seen as green. However, special naturally occurring conditions will create distortions in the crystal structure that takes place during growth will be seen in the diamond from light pink to deep pink to red. Red diamonds are extremely rare, much more than colorless, and they are the most expensive. This section was just meant to give you a quick peek into the chemistry and spectroscopy of diamonds. This is a very complex and confusing subject full of exceptions and special terms and symbols, and quite frankly, that's the aspect I like the least about diamonds.

This leads me to my next point. Whatever happens inside the diamond, whichever way the light is being reflected back to the observer is in direct relation to the *state of being* inside that diamond. The same goes for us human beings. Whatever happens outside of us is a direct reflection of our internal states of being. With that in mind, you can conclude that we are 100% responsible for what happens to us, whether good or bad, because it came out as a reflection from within us. The point of origin of the reflection is like a seed. The seed is always the origin, and the fruit is the result. Whatever you have planted in your mind, whatever you hold in your mind, whether deliberately or unconsciously, will soon manifest outside and produce a result. And that's exactly the reason why we need to purify ourselves on a regular basis. The nature of the fruit is a reflection of the seed. The nature of the action is a reflection of the thought. What is the nature of the thought? We better make sure it's a good thought, a good seed! Once you have rid your system of the unwanted negative stuff, you create a sort of a vacuum and allow room for new and clean energy. Hence, you can allow Divine Light to work its way into your life. You move the curtain over to the side and open the windows to allow clean, fresh air and sunshine into your house. It's the same with human beings and the mind. Everything is a reflection.

I remember many years ago a lady came to see me in the hopes of selling her diamond. It was an Oval set in a simple gold ring. She asked if I could make her an offer.

"It's a beautiful diamond. How come you want to sell it?" I asked.

That's a risky question to ask. You never know what reaction you'll get. Most of the time, people have no idea about the value of their diamonds, and because they've put a lot sentimental value on them, they end up thinking it's worth a lot more than their true market values. So when you give them a quote, some people panic or think you're trying to rob them. This is not my approach. I've always seen diamonds as beautiful no matter what and always wanted to share my appreciation with people in the hope that they would see the same things. In this case, it was a home run. She replied;

"I don't like it. I never did. Ever since my husband got it for me I can see a spot inside close to the middle. Look! It's right there, and it drives me crazy. So I want to sell it and buy another one with the money, and I don't want him to know!"

When she handed the ring over, I looked at the diamond, and sure enough, the inclusion was visible without any effort. But there was something very different about that inclusion. It had a glow, a green glow. Yes, it was very small, but I have amazing vision when it comes to diamonds and it was very easy for me, what can I say! But I always confirm with my loupe to make sure I'm not hallucinating. The inclusion in this diamond was a type I had seen only in theories and only in very few books I had studied. Although I had no actual way to determine the real nature of it because it is inside the diamond, it

I described it as Green Garnet, but I maybe it was green diopside. It's naturally occurring, but it's an extremely rare inclusion found in diamonds. Garnets grow in the similar environments as diamonds so this is how that conclusion is drawn. I had seen red inclusions, also described as Garnet, once while taking a course at GIA labs in 1995, and I've seen very few more since in my career. But the green was a new one. That was my first one in 2006. The only other one I've seen was in a 2.32ct H SI2 round brilliant in 2014. There were two of them next to each other. It was fascinating! I continued;

"Let's dig a little deeper and investigate, shall we?"

Then I walked toward the microscope. She looked at me with a strange face, I swear she thought I was a little nuts. I must have looked like a mad scientist, who knows? I spent about forty-five minutes with this lady. We went over everything on this diamond—the rarity, the nature, and the odds of finding such a diamond much less owning one. To make it easier for her to see it clearly, I put it under the microscope with a 40x magnification and changed the angle of observation in what is called "dark field" illumination. By the way, "dark field" illumination with a microscope refers to light coming from the bottom with the top light turned off. This allows the color of the inclusion, among many other things, to be seen with the light passing through it instead of reflecting off it.

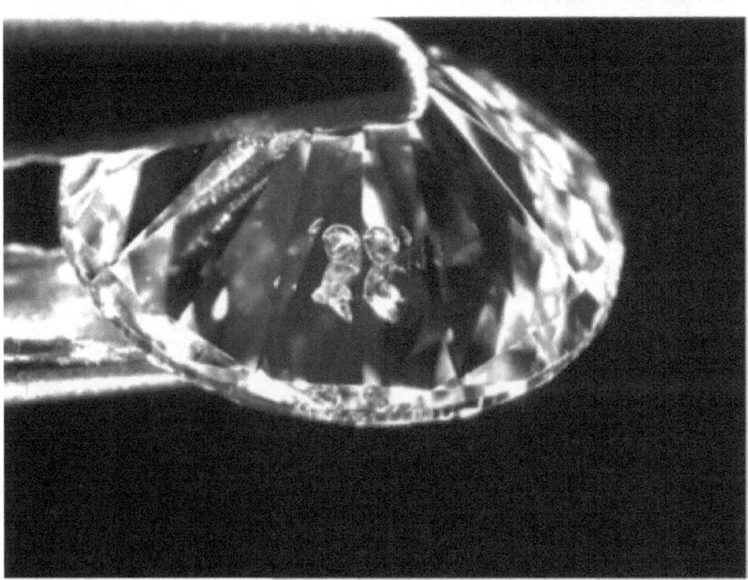

Photo courtesy of AGS Laboratories
(Photographer: Jennifer Tobiasson).

                                             Yvan Kaprielian

She was utterly astounded and fascinated by her diamond. After seeing the color and understanding the inclusion, and after I pointed it out her, when I took it away from the microscope she was still able to see the green of the inclusion.

Then I said;

"Lady, this is a very rare inclusion you have in your diamond, especially one this big. I've been in the diamond industry for fifteen years. It's the first time I see one. I only knew of these in theory, not in real life. As you now know, when it comes to diamonds it's all about rarity. I can promise you no one you know or anyone you'll come across will have this type of diamond. It is as rare, as unique, and as precious as your marriage. Now that you know the nature and rarity of your diamond, cherish it, don't ever sell it, and don't ever let anyone talk you out of it."

She had tears in her eyes, and she said that she had thought her husband had just gotten her a crappy and cheap diamond. She hugged me, thanked me a thousand times, promised me she'd never sell it, and walked out.

You see, not all inclusions are bad. So you might ask, "If it's so rare, why isn't it valued and sold accordingly?" In the diamond industry, inclusions are inclusions. When buying a diamond, you're buying the diamond, not the inclusions. Diamonds are valued for the lack of inclusions, not their respective nature, and inclusions always have a negative impact on the value. But every now and then with proper guidance and expertise, some lucky people end up with diamond inclusions that are a lot more rare than flawless diamonds. They are marvels and miracles of nature.

Look, be smart, and don't beat yourself up over the head because you're seeing your flaws. They are not all bad! They are not all obstacles blocking Light. The point I want to make is that what society wants us to see as flaws or labeled as impediments could actually be some of your biggest stepping stones—if you change the angle of observation! It's a choice you have to *decide* to make.

Take me as an example. As you've read at the beginning of my book, English is not my first language. It's not my second language either. It's my third. First is Armenian, and second is French. When I first started speaking English, I had a massive accent that I didn't like. I thought it was important for me to assimilate in the American culture and learn to speak English as an American. When I moved to the United States and started high school, the kids made fun of me every time I said something. That's probably why I didn't like my accent. They pretended they could not understand me, or maybe they really didn't understand me. I don't really know. But it was the way they responded that was really difficult for me. They humiliated me and rejected me, and for the most part, they didn't accept me in their so-called groups. They called me the *frog*. I learned years later that they used that term because people in France eat frog legs. I never did, but apparently, frog tastes like chicken. I always liked to joke around, that's in my nature. But I hated it when they made fun of me in that way because I knew it was not just to play around. So I got into fights over it. Hey, what did you expect? I was fourteen and fifteen years old back then! So I didn't talk much after a while, afraid people would make fun of me again and again. I didn't get to practice my English much other than times with my cousins and some close friends in my community. But I didn't realize what an impact it had on my psyche until I addressed this problem, this flaw. It was like having PTSD! This led me to understand why I became so knowledgeable on the subject of diamonds later in life. I didn't really get to actually speak English properly until a few years after high school and after I started working at the age of seventeen. The fact that I had to use my elementary English-speaking level to explain diamonds to clients made it easy for them to understand such a technical and difficult product to buy. I call it the "blind item." You're buying it completely blindly, and you know practically nothing about it. It gave me the biggest edge over other professionals. By changing the angle of observation, I was able to turn what I originally thought was a massive obstacle into a massive stepping stone. But I was willing to face the hard facts and the fears, and I had to build up enough courage and strength to lift my foot high enough to turn this blockage into a stepping stone. What I thought was my biggest weakness turned out to be my biggest strength—just one step in front of me. Had I not done that, who knows if you would be reading this book right now?

Think about what you see as obstacles, as flaws, currently in your life right now. How can you change the angle of observation and turn these into stepping stones? How much could you improve your situation with just one step up?

Chapter VIII
The Filters

There's another important part of my Diamond analogy that I must share with you—I call them the filters. Of course, there are many different types of filters in this world. However, the ones I'll be referring to are the "optical filters" for the simple fact that they are related directly to light and diamonds. In the realm of photography, filters are used to alter and enhance the moment being photographed. For example, to accentuate the colors of a sunset or a sunrise, you can use colored filters. You can use a polarizer to eliminate unwanted glass or water surface reflections. My brother, Stephen, was a big fan of old-school photography. You know, the type of cameras that use 24 exposure films that have to be developed in a dark room with red light? Remember those? Some of you readers are too young to know about them, and that's fine. You have to live in your time, and in this day and age, everything is digital. And since you can easily manipulate digital images, filters may not be used as much. My brother had many different types of filters, and my favorite one was the polarizer. We used to go by lakes, rivers, and ponds to take photos of the fishes using the polarizing filter and eliminating all of the reflections so that we could actually see through the water. That was so cool! By rotating the filter back and forth, the reflections would disappear and reappear. Reflection… No reflection… Reflection… No reflection… G's, wonder why I liked that? One time—I think it was in the early 90s—we drove to Weehawken, New Jersey, by the old wooden docks. These were basically abandoned and totally degraded. They were also fenced in and totally closed off to the public. But of course, given the crazy adventurers we were, we jumped over and walked all the way to the end, at the edge. That was really dangerous. The docks were in really bad shape with sections literally caved in or missing altogether. Despite the danger, we had the best view on the Manhattan skyline, and we were determined to capture the Twin Towers on film. It was such a clear and beautiful night. We both loved those Towers. It's a shame what happened there on 9/11, and I really miss seeing that unique and amazing skyline.

We took such magnificent shots. My brother taught me a lot about photography. I wanted to do my own experiments, so one day I grabbed a few of his colored filters and took them to work with me. I had lights, and I had diamonds, so I started to play and experiment. I used daylight florescent tube lights, held a diamond in my tweezers with my right hand, rocking it back and forth to catch the flashes and reflections of light. Then I held the filters with my other hand, placing them between the light and the diamond and switched the filters every now and then. It was interesting to see how the diamond reflected colored filtered light in its various parts.

As a side note, there are different facet families in a diamond. Let me show you. From the top down, we start with the Table, a single octagonal (eight-sided) facet from which extends the next 8 triangular facets called the Star facets. They are called Star facet because they actually form a star. Next, there are the 8 Bezel facets, which are kite-shaped and extend from the Table on the upper tip of the kite and are located adjacent to the Star facets down to the Girdle. The next set of facets is called the Upper Girdle

                                                                                 Yvan Kaprielian

facets. There are 16 of them, and they extend halfway up to the Table. The outline or the perimeter of the diamond is called the Girdle. Sometimes the Girdle is not faceted, and sometimes it is and if so, they are never counted. Usually, on higher quality diamonds, it is faceted or at the very least polished. Unpolished and unfaceted Girdles tend to look white and frosty just like a piece of tumbled glass on the beach. The next set is called the Lower Girdle facets. There are 16 and they are the counterpart of the Upper Girdle facets. They should be aligned at the exact opposite of one another. They start at the Girdle and usually extend 80% of the way down the pavilion. The last family of 8 is called Pavilion Mains. They extend from the Girdle to the Culet. They are also kite-shaped, and these are the counterparts of the Bezel facets and should be aligned at the exact opposite from one another. And of course, that's assuming the diamond is well cut and well proportioned.

Here is the diagram so you can visual this.

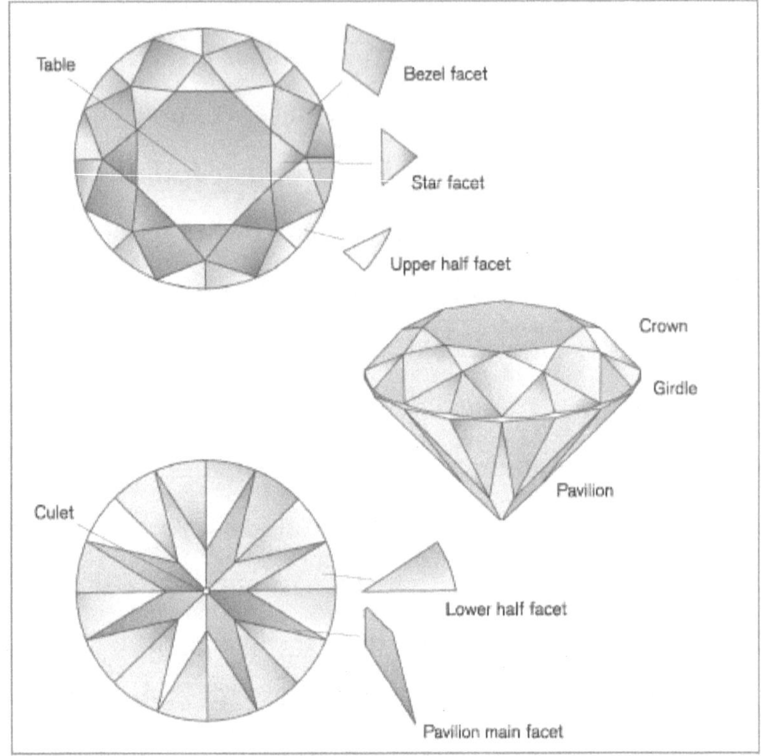

Photo courtesy of GIA (Gemological Institute of America)

By the way, this is one way to evaluate how well the diamond is cut. By understanding this concept, you can observe the symmetry of the facet families.

Maybe you've heard of the reference "Hearts and Arrows" to describe diamonds? There's a beautiful pattern of evenly spread-out look-alike hearts and arrows that becomes visible when the cut of the diamond has reached perfect symmetry. Unless you are trained to see this, it requires a special tool. Can you guess what this tool is composed of? You guessed it—a colored filter!

The following photos show what this tool looks like. The red filter is on the viewer and can be interchanged with the blue. The next photo shows the diamond face down to see the hearts, and the last photo has the diamond face up to see the arrows.

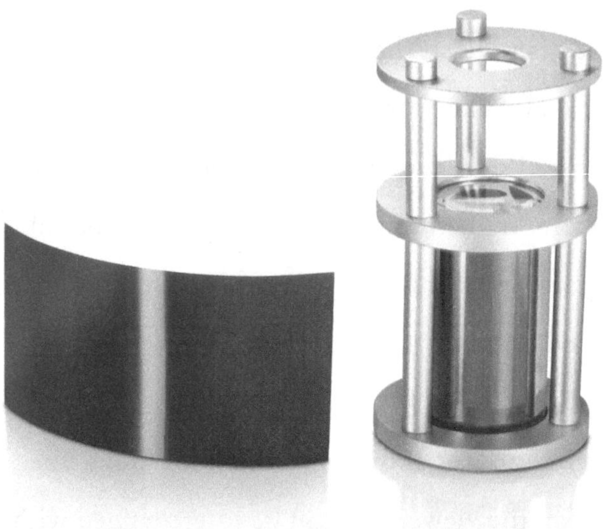

The viewer

Face down view

Face up view

The diamond is centered on one end of a small glass cylinder with the filter totally covering the tube so that the majority of the light passing through is filtered, and a magnifier on the other end is used to facilitate viewing the patterns. The most common filter color is red. Why red? Because it colors the diamond in red and makes it more romantic and makes the observer feel love, perhaps? Consumers love that corny stuff. No! It's simply because red gives a great contrast so that we can see the patterns. The other common color is blue. You may ask, "So is the blue for when you're feeling blue?" That's funny. I don't know. I don't think so! I suppose it gives a great contrast too.

After developing my Diamond analogy, I revisited that day when I was playing with the filters, and I thought; "*How does this relate to our lives?*" I got an answer practically immediately. I didn't have to wait for years this time around, thank God. I thought; *"What if these filters are representing thoughts, habits, patterns, belief systems, and mental programs?"* If we really look at our lives as diamonds receiving Light, then the filters are obstructing the Light to a certain degree. Therefore, the Light received is already tinted before it is refracted and reflected. In turn, the Light sent back out is filtered and tinted accordingly and respectively to one or more of these filters. Mind you, this is in addition to the inclusions. The filters are outside, affecting the Light before it enters the diamond, and inclusions are inside, affecting the light before it exits the diamond. Can you see the connection?

Many people have asked me over the years, "How are the hearts and arrows formed?" That's a great and interesting question! They are formed by reflection patterns of the various facet families. The Hearts are reflections of the Pavilion facets, and they are visible when the diamond is observed with the Table down. The Arrows are also reflections of the Pavilion facets, and they are visible from the center all the way through the Bezel facets when the diamond is observed Table up, giving birth to a different pattern of reflections. So what's the big deal? In the world we know that arrows are used to point to a direction. In the case of diamonds, and to be aligned with my analogy, the arrows are pointing at the hearts. You can also say that from the Table-up view, the arrows are pointing outward from the center, from the heart of the diamond. So whichever way you look at it, they are either pointing at the heart or originate from the heart. In spiritual terms, the heart is always at the center of everything. Everything starts from the heart. Everything has to come out from the heart. If everything we did had heart energy, our lives, our society, this world would be a much better place. Once again, the diamond is clearly a messenger.

Here is an image to show you what I mean.

Photo courtesy of IGI (International Gemological Institute

Perhaps this should have been the first chapter. Changing filters or removing them altogether is critical, but the reason why I place here is because I wanted to give you a foundation for what's expressed in the next pages.

So let's take a look at our thoughts. Thoughts are real and have a consciousness of their own. We create thoughts every day, and according to Dr. Joe Dispenza, one of favorite researcher and expert on the functions of the brain, we create sixty to seventy thousand thoughts per day on average. But 90% of these are the same ones as the day before. And we are only aware of about two thousand of them on average. That's less than 3%. So it's obvious that we function predominantly from an unconscious and automatic state of mind with unconscious programs, patterns, beliefs systems, and habits. As I explained in a previous chapter, I believe that everything we do is significant. When something happens to us, whether significant or seemingly insignificant, unless we make a conscious and deliberate effort to see how we react to a given situation then that situation in question gets labeled by an automatic mental pattern that is in alignment with our mental program or belief system at that time. And that situation remains labeled that way until it is addressed, if it is ever addressed. This relates to the *flaws* described earlier. In this case, this particular situation gets labeled a *flaw* and becomes a blockage. Does this make sense? Ever heard the phrase "It's not what happens to you, it's how you react to it that matters." Well, this is exactly my point.

Master Choa goes in great detail about thought forms, how they are created, their energy aspect, and the effect they have on each and every one of us. When you generate a thought, it is created in a form or an energy ball, so to speak. That thought form remains in what is called your aura or your energy field, if you prefer. Positive things as well as the negative ones tend to stick around and stay there. The sad part is that we also tend to pick up thought forms from all around us. Napoleon Hill makes this clear in his book *Think and Grow Rich* that this is real and true. These thoughts are vibrational in nature, and they can be attracted or attract thoughts of a similar vibrational frequency. This is also known as the Law of Attraction. Have you ever come home after a long commute and just felt angry or sad or depressed for no apparent reason? Have ever had a conversation with someone sad, depressed, or angry in person or over the phone and started feeling that way too shortly afterward? Have you gotten together with a group of happy people when you were feeling down and started feeling great and having fun all of a sudden? Remember the first story I told you in the introduction about the client who said that I must feel really fulfilled every time I sell an engagement ring? I was wondering if he had picked up on my thoughts or if I picked up on his. Master Choa teaches the many different levels of truth in regards to these statements.

In Pranic Healing, there are multiple ways to cleanse your aura from negative thoughts and replace them with wholesome and positive energies. The concept of energy is taught in great details. It's probably the most comprehensive and powerful yet simplest teachings in the world. I was introduced to Pranic Healing in 2001, and I've been practicing it ever since then. I'm lucky to say I learned quite a bit about energy, and with my current state of consciousness I know I'm only scratching the surface. There's so much to know. However, I have met many people who have been certified from various energy healing modalities for much longer than me and some who have studied energy for a greater part of their lives, and they have made Pranic Healing their main practice. Dr. Glenn Mendoza, MD, who is also one of my mentors, is one of the top physicians in the United States. He is a practicing neonatologist in New York, an associate clinical professor in pediatrics at New York Medical College, and a receiver of prestigious awards for medical achievements in the area of pediatrics and neonatal care. He is the president of the Center for Pranic Healing in New Jersey, a Master Pranic Healer, and one of the senior disciples of Grandmaster Choa Kok Sui. His wife, Marilag Mendoza, is also a senior disciple. They don't follow and practice the teachings just because they sound good. By understanding energy and applying these teachings, you build a bridge with an HOV lane to higher spiritual development called Arhatic Yoga.

One easy and very effective way to cleanse your energy system is through meditation. Grand Master Choa formulated a meditation called Twin Hearts Meditation, also known as Planetary Meditation for Peace. It is currently practiced by hundreds of thousands of people around the world from all walks of life and all religions. It is called Twin Hearts because it activates the two heart centers. The first is the Heart center (aka the heart chakra) located at the physical heart level. This is where love and affection for the people we know and love is experienced. The second heart is located on top of your head, and it's called the Crown center (aka crown chakra). This is where higher love for humanity as a whole is experienced. The activation and opening of the Crown allows for a greater downpour of Divine energy and Divine Light and consequently can circulate through your systems. Let me just point out and remind you here that the top part of the diamond where the majority of the light enters and comes out is called the Crown. By raising your hands at chest level with your palms facing out, you allow this Divine energy to continue circulating and exiting through your hands. At the same time you recited the prayer of Saint Francis of Assisi and allow yourself to become a channel and a Divine instrument of peace, love, forgiveness, faith, hope, Light and joy. By envisioning the Earth in front of you the size of a soccer ball the energy is then transformed into blessings. The circulation of this energy has a great cleansing, soothing, and calming effect on your system. You will feel it almost immediately, and you will feel peace. When your aura is free from all these thought forms, whether they are yours or not, the chatter in your mind stops temporarily. In the middle of the meditation there's an Om chanting followed by a period of silence. Both are very important. At the end of the meditation you may feel you have an excess of energy. You can use that Divine energy and project it onto your family, your friends, your job, your projects and so on.

You will most likely feel an immediate positive difference, even with only one meditation. When practiced regularly, over the course of a few months or maybe weeks, depending on your degree of development, you will see substantial positive changes in the way you feel and react. And those changes, when you work on improving yourself in parallel, can become permanent.

I do this meditation regularly for many years. I can testify that it works great, and I would recommend it to anyone. If you are under eighteen, however, you should ask your parents to contact a Pranic Healing center and seek for guidance. If you have high blood pressure or any heart condition, contact a center for Pranic Healing near you and seek advice.

I certainly hope that you have noticed this meditation is based on the hearts. Everything has to start with the heart and go outward from the heart. There are many benefits to this meditation and many levels of understanding as well, some of which are taught in the higher courses of Arhatic Yoga. You can look for centers near you where this meditation is offered for free, and you can buy the guided meditation on CD from Pranic Healing websites. The meditation is only twenty minutes. That's twenty minutes to feel better and be at peace just by closing your eyes and breathing. Sometimes you have to wait that long to get your morning coffee at your local coffee shops. The choice is yours, so choose wisely.

To get more information go to:

www.meditationontwinhearts.com

Chapter IX
The Teachers

From the day we are born to the day we die, we are in a constant learning mode, or least we are supposed to be. We encounter many teachers in our lifetimes. Usually, the first teachers we have are our parents. Our parents also had their teachers throughout their lifetime. At each cycle, values are taught and transmitted, and in turn, these values are passed down from generation to generation. The younger generation always inherits the good values of the previous ones, but also inherits the values that are not necessarily good that new generation. Each new generation is different in terms of evolution, consciousness, and society as a whole. The Internet is very recent in our world, about 20 years maybe a little more. Think about the people who were born and never knew what it was like to not have the Internet for communication? Don't you think their values will be different from their parents' when it comes to communication? Some core values will always apply, of course—respecting the beliefs of others and the Golden Rule, "Don't do or say to others what you wouldn't want said or done onto you." Then there are values taught in schools, the ones that come directly from teachers and professors, and those from fellow students as well. Interactions with other people can teach us new lessons and inevitably, followed closely by the general lessons we learn from society once we get in the world of jobs. We also have religious teachers. Regardless of which denomination of religion, values and beliefs are taught and reinforced again and again. Somehow these values tend to become deeply embedded and anchored in our minds. Why? Perhaps they are tapping into a realm of our life they call spirituality, this seemingly mysterious part of our consciousness, the so-called teachings from those initiates, privileged ones, or spiritual leaders. Or Perhaps because these teachings may be based on concepts which we cannot grasp, or see, or be evaluated or be measured by modern science? Although today these assumptions may not be entirely true anymore. With the use of computerized technologies, the effect of meditation can actually be measured by the various electrical impulses created by the brain. We can evaluate which part of the brain is being activated and what effect the meditation has on the overall being of the person. The Twin Hearts Meditation actually shows amazing results when scientifically observed and evaluated.

We are constantly influenced by our surroundings, our environments, what we watch on TV, what we read in the papers, what we watch on the news in the morning and again repeated at night, and what we choose to click on when surfing the Web. Ever since I was a kid, I never believed what I saw or heard from the media. I thought; *"How do I know if what they are saying is true? How come they are saying one thing on one channel and something different on another?"* And you know, in France in the late 70s and early 80s, you could count the number of TV channels on one hand. We are led to believe that the news is true because of the words *reporter* and *journalist* are associated with the broadcasts. They are supposed to report and write about events as they happened and not give their opinions. Today we know that nothing could be further from the truth than what is being reported in the mainstream media around the world. Be very careful what you choose to believe when listening or reading the news. Don't just blindly believe what is being said or shown on TV about national and international events because someone or a network said so. Research and evaluate for yourself before drawing any conclusions.

> *"Accept something only when you*
>
> *have validated it for yourself."*
>
> *~ Grand Master Choa Kok Sui ~*
>
> *(Teaching according to the Lord Buddha)*

Values and beliefs change or get reinforced again once you get married and have children—that is, if you choose that path for your life. All these values and beliefs influence our decision-making process and affect our life. And most of the time, if we are not aware, these values and beliefs can change without us even noticing.

Then you have values and beliefs that are self-realized. This means that when we experience an event, depending on the outcome, we draw certain conclusions. These conclusions are usually based on how we see and label things, and we label and see things based on our values and beliefs. So you just went full circle. Some people call it the vicious circle. At this point, you can make a choice. You can choose to create a new starting point. You can either reinforce the value being expressed or question its validity. The interesting thing is that it's easier to change when you're younger, depending on your life experience. When you grow older, your convictions also grow stronger, which makes it harder for you to change. So it's a catch-22. When you're young, you are carefree, nothing can affect you and feel you have plenty of time ahead of you, so who cares? When you're older, you either feel comfortable because you think you know everything and you've done everything or you may feel it's too late to make a change. So what do we do? The key is to remain open-minded and understand that *we don't understand* everything. When do we start? The best time to start is *NOW*. There's always another way to look

                                    Yvan Kaprielian

at everything; as many as they are people on the planet and apparently it's increasing very rapidly.

Have you ever looked up in the sky and saw faces, animals, or shapes in the clouds? Have you ever pointed them out to people next to you but they could not find what you could see? Why is that? It was so clear to you, but no one else could see it. You can take one gemstone, give it independently to five different jewelers with gemology degrees, and have them identify it. Guess what! You'll get five different answers—that is, unless there's a specific rule to follow. For example, an electronic scale can be used to measure the carat weight, and that measurement can't be argued. Well, some people may be so deeply embedded in their convictions that they would find a way to say there was something wrong with the scale. Anything that is left to the opinion of a person will always vary from person to person. Clarity characteristics in diamonds cannot be evaluated with a machine, only by the trained human eye with certain specific guidelines. For example, when SI2 or a lower-clarity grade is assessed on a diamond, it means that without the aid of a 10x loupe, the inclusions are visible to the naked eye. But whose eye? Yours as a consumer or the trained grader's? I've had clients who could see VS2 clarity characteristics without magnification, and I've had clients who could not find SI2 inclusions under the microscope at 20x magnification. At my best, when grading conditions were proper, I could find VS1 clarity characteristics without a loupe. So who's right? Well, in my book there's no right or wrong. There are only opinions and varying degrees of abilities. The lady who wanted to sell her diamond with that green inclusion didn't see the green in it until I pointed it out. She only saw a dark spot. I showed her how to appreciate her diamond, and she never looked at it the same way again. She had hated it for years, and forty-five minutes after she visited me, she walked out loving it. So if we stay open to seeing things in a different way, we give ourselves the opportunity to grow. I was exposed to so many different aspects of the diamond industry, learning so much from so many different people. It opened me up to seeing and experiencing things in different ways, different than most people. Outside my work I also took massive steps to learn new ways to see and experience life. I looked at the values and the beliefs that I had gotten from my parents, schools, society, and church, and I asked myself if all these were serving me. Did they improve my life? If so, how? If not, why? I had to stay open in order to receive the answers. And answers I got!

I met many different teachers throughout my life, some I have explicitly made references to in this book and some I have not. But one thing is for sure. They've all altered the way I look at my life, my work, society, and humanity as a whole. They helped me change the angles of my observation. As I've mentioned in the early parts of this book, I was heavily invested in the church for more than twelve years when I was younger, yet during that time I learned very little about the essence of my Being and my spiritual evolution. Lots of questions were left unanswered, and somehow, I had to figure it all out on my own. And a great deal of these teachings are fear-based. Granted, that's a part of our evolution process—to learn and figure stuff out on our own. But no one or very few who have advanced significantly in their development did it on their own. There's always a greater Teacher involved to some degree.

I remember when I was younger, my grandpa used to take me on walks around the villages, the fields, and the forests. This happened in the late 1970s in the greater suburbs of Paris. He used to teach me his values—values he got form his dad and past generations. I learned many good things, such as basic survival stuff, what to enjoy and admire, and also what to look out for in nature. He also taught me some strange things about life, things that made me laugh later on in life after understanding the basic principles. He repeated so many times over and over again;

"Yvan, if you do bad things and if you're not nice, Father God will throw a rock at you from up above!"

Can you image what went through my mind as a kid? Even my dad reinforced that belief from time to time. What kind of messed-up belief is that? But, if my grandpa and dad said so then it must be true, right? When we are kids, we always look up to our parents for guidance and to our grandparents for wisdom. By human nature, males tend to bond together, and the same is true for females. So I thought if my father and my grandfather said this then, it must be true. Think about how easy it is to impress a belief on a five-year-old kid with a vivid imagination. I was looking at them with my eyes open wide in awe and absorbing everything without any conscious filtering, taking in every word of the story literally. That belief got directly imprinted in the subconscious mind and soon to play a major role in influencing my thinking and reaction processes, labeling accordingly the various events in my life. And the scary part is that I would not even be aware of it anymore after a while. We are taught by religious leaders and reinforced in movies and literature that there's a mysterious man called God who's dressed in a white robe and who has a long white beard and some kind of a scepter jumping from clouds to clouds. And he's supposed to watch over me, protect me, and love me. Now in my five-year-old mind, why would this all-powerful man throw a rock at me the moment I did or said something bad? How screwed up of a belief that is! Sounds so Hollywood, right?! Now associate this with the fear of all fears— death! A rock falling from the sky and landing on your head would definitely kill you, this means death. These are two massively conflicting teachings. On one side he protects you and loves you and the other story tells you if you step out of line, you're dead. Not knowing any better at that age, those two stories and the fear got connected and made sense to me. So I drew my own conclusion based on the false evidence and ultimately choose to label that belief as true. But the really screwed-up thing about this is that it was all happening unconsciously at such a very young age.

So I asked my grandpa;

"What if there are no clouds. Where does he go?"

The answer was always;

"It doesn't matter. He's Father God, and he can do anything he wants."

Of course! No real answer! Go figure!

Don't you have a few stories like that? Think about what you were taught when you were young. Do these stories

                                                  Yvan Kaprielian

make any sense today? And these stories can obviously vary depending on your cultural heritage.

The Law of Karma is not fatalistic. It gives you the ability to create your future. By planting the right seed, you harvest the right crop.

~ Grand Master Choa Kok Sui ~

I learned later on in life that this story was nothing more than a symbolic tale referring to the Law of Karma. So why can't they just explain that word for word and stop teaching in parables? If you do good things, good things will happen to you. If you do bad things, bad things will happen to you. That's it! How hard was that? In these terms then, no one can deny that whatever you do, good or bad, is a direct reflection to your thoughts and actions. Hence, as

I have expressed in earlier chapters, we are 100% responsible for what happens to us—period, end of that story! The idea that some evil spook wants to hurt us or give us a hard time is, in my opinion, nothing more than socially accepted beliefs to point the finger outward and blame everything in the world, whether visible or not visible, but ourselves.

"It's not my fault!"

"I didn't bring this in my life!"

"I didn't ask for this!" "That's his/her fault!" "He/she did it, it wasn't me!" "I have nothing to do with this!"

These excuses are some of the easiest ways to remain in complete denial and refuse to take responsibility and control of our thoughts and actions. It's so much easier to point the finger at something or someone else instead of pointing at the mirror. Again, as I pointed it out earlier, lots of people want to improve and change their situations and circumstances, but only a few are willing to change themselves. Now that I have made you a little more aware through my Diamond analogy, see it and experience it through yourself.

"Where religion stops is where

true spirituality starts."

~ Yvan Kaprielian ~

All these confusing parables and misleading stories changed dramatically for me in 2001 after I met Master Choa. This was shortly after I had left the church altogether and had decided to seek other ways to evolve spiritually. My great friend Joanne introduced me to Pranic Healing and GMCKS's teachings. She knew I was searching for a different spiritual path. She said;

"Yvan, just come and see if this is for you. The things I'm learning are really amazing, and the people are great. Just come one evening. I go every Wednesday night. If you don't like it, I'll never mention it again… Promise!"

She had been telling me about it for more than six months. Finally, after some resistance, I decided to go. My first Twin Hearts Meditation was very interesting and intriguing. That was when I first met Dr. Glenn. The group was very easy going, and the people started sharing jokes with one another. I was still resisting and feeling tense, so Joanne told me to share some of my jokes, which really loosened me up. They actually thought some of my jokes were funny, can you believe it? I liked it. When we laugh, we release a lot of negative emotional charge; it opens the heart and makes it easier to meditate. The atmosphere was lovely, but most importantly, what I experienced during the meditation is what pulled me to go back the following week. I saw and experienced things during the meditation that I had been seeing since I was a little kid right before I would fall asleep. Yes, the group was super welcoming and fun, but it was my experience during the Twin Hearts meditation that blew my mind. I thought; *"Perhaps this could be the way to get the answers I've been looking for?"* Forgive me, but for your own sake, I am not going to share with you what I saw and experienced. When we mediate, the experience is very personal, it's very unique to our Being, and each meditation is different. My sharing with you might lead you to have expectations, and when you start meditating with expectations, you'll end up meditating on the expectation, which defeats the purpose of the meditation in the

                    Yvan Kaprielian

first place. And if that expectation isn't met, you won't get to enjoy the meditation and miss out on your own experience.

If I ever meet you in the future after you've done some meditating, I would be happy to share my experience and hear about yours as well. But for the time being have no expectations. Just do it! A month later I attended a higher course workshop, and that was when I met Master Choa. He actually sat down with me after a lecture and genuinely wanted to get to know me. From that point on, somehow I knew this was going to be a major stepping stone in my personal and spiritual development. Let me introduce you to him and give you a short synopsis of his life.

"When the student is ready to listen and learn
the Teacher appears"

~ Many Great Teachers ~

Master Choa Kok Sui (1952–2007) is the founder of Modern Pranic Healing and Arhatic Yoga. He also was a scientist, a teacher, a healer, a philanthropist, and an author. Through his research and experiments, he developed a comprehensive method of cleansing and energizing the energy system that permeates the physical body, thereby accelerating the rate at which the body can heal itself.

Yvan Kaprielian

He demonstrated that energy is an important factor in healing the physical as well as the psyche. In the world of the sciences, he was a chemical engineer, which led him to carefully develop, test and replicate techniques which encompass this modality. Through extensive research, experimentation, and validation, he cultivated the science and art of Pranic Healing, which offers the ideal balance of science and spirituality for holistic health and success. Through his pragmatic teaching methodology, his students are able to obtain relevant lessons in a relatively short period of time. The combination of his experience and wisdom as a father, self-made successful businessman, adept scientist, and spiritual teacher are palpable in the way that Pranic Healing addresses the real needs of people on a daily basis. The dynamic style of Grand Master Choa Kok Sui's teaching is reflected in the direct, uncluttered style of his writing. By reading his books, one rapidly gains insight into the principles of life energy and their modern-day applications, such as healing, good health, emotional balance, mental clarity, spiritual growth, and an abundant life. By rediscovering many ancient and esoteric *secrets* and understanding their daily applications in life, practitioners find themselves enjoying life more fully with less stress and greater fulfillment. He wrote and published twenty books that have been translated into twenty-seven languages. These cover topics that include healing, spirituality, and psychic self-defense. And for those seeking to be on the higher spiritual path, Grand Master Choa developed Arhatic Yoga, a system of nonsectarian practices that leads to greater soul (or self) realization. These fantastic yogic practices from many traditions use ancient technology in original and creative combinations to activate and align the chakra system or energy centers and to awaken the *kundalini energy* or the sacred fire. Though Grand Master Choa Kok Sui often said he was not born a healer, he became through his constant research and love for humanity a true master of energy. On all five continents, Grand Master Choa offered to use his time to heal attendees within the class and their loved ones. Many were healed instantly from chronic ailments, both physical and psychological. The degree of proficiency achieved during his lifetime is remarkable and an inspiration to all those who are interested in the healing arts. He was also a great philanthropist. Grand Master Choa was born in a wealthy family, yet his heart was filled with compassion and generosity for those who suffered from pain, poverty, and a lack of education. Through the global mission of Pranic Healing, Grand Master Choa established several humanitarian projects to feed the hungry and also provide help to the sick and those in need of medical attention. He ensured that all the funds actually went to help those in need instead of covering operational costs. This ingenious approach has given thousands of Pranic Healers around the world the opportunity to partake in healing the communities they live in, thereby making the world a better place. These healers can also experience the bliss that comes from serving others in need. He had an amazing way of explaining extremely complex subjects in the realm of spirituality, many from various religious and spiritual origins, and making them simple enough to understand for everybody. I could fully relate to that because I felt I could do the same with the complexities in my field, the diamond world. It was through much of his teachings that I was able to solidify my Diamond analogy. The many questions and scattered theories I had developed were all over the place in my mind. Many of the realizations I've had and many of the ones I have expressed in this book took place after I met him and started following his teachings and meditations. He is a great spiritual Teacher, and I can't thank him enough for that. He demystified all the stories and parables from religious teachings and explained what they actually meant, their correlations to our lives, and how to apply their lessons in order to improve and move forward in every aspect of our lives. The details were so simple, and they didn't take very long to explain. Truths are always simple and short.

Grand Master Choa also had his Teacher, a Teacher greater than himself from whom he has learned. We'll just leave it at that for now.

I also have a mentor who has been instrumental at helping me stay on the right track. His name is Gerry. Interestingly enough, he just so happens to be in the diamond industry. Although he never mentions it publically, I know he has mentored many people to either open them to this path or help them stay on it. And he, too, had his teacher and mentor. We have known each other for more than twenty years, but it's only in the past five years that we actually connected on the spiritual level. I suppose this took place only when I was ready to continue listening and learning.

I said earlier "When the student is ready, the teacher will appear." Spiritual teachings can't be forced onto people. They have to be ready and willing to learn.

Meeting Master Choa in 2001 was exactly what I was looking for, exactly what I needed, and the event came exactly when I was ready to learn. Just like a rough diamond, a master cutter found me and picked me up and showed me how to understand my-self and make a masterpiece out of my life. And that's a work in progress.

NOTES

Chapter X
Now What?

Well, we have traveled quite a bit in this book. We have bounced back and forth in so many ways, exploring diamonds and exploring our present and past lives. We took a quick glimpse into our possible future, making connections and creating parallels. But the question remains. What are you going to do now that you know all this? Will you starting making changes? At least small ones?! No? Why not? It's hard to turn back once you know that everything in your life right now is a product of your creation. Will you continue to point your finger out and away from the mirror? Will you continue to blame everything and everyone else around you? Or will you start to turn to the mirror and turn inward? Will you take full responsibility for your actions and accept the results?

Look around you, my friend! Look at what's happening in the world. Everything seems so uncertain, unstable, and unpredictable. Many of our points of reference are changing so rapidly, and some are disappearing altogether.

Have you ever been indoor rock climbing? Artificial walls with preset grips are really cool and so much fun. It's a great exercise on both a physical and mental level. You have to plan how to climb according to the grips that specific wall offers, and there are also different skill levels. You also have to be physically prepared for that too if you want to reach the top. Now, imagine if all of the grips started to randomly move and change positions or kept moving when you were a quarter of the way up the wall. What if some disappeared altogether? How would you do? Would you make it to the top? If you didn't, how long would you hold before you ran out of strength and fell? Is there something in place to catch you when you fall? And if you did stay on the wall, how much longer would it take to reach the top? What would be the physical and mental toll you'd have to pay? The grips on the wall are like our points of reference in life. Imagine if your go-to points of reference, the ones you are accustomed to grip or hold on to, kept changing, moving around, or disappearing. How would you do in life? Ever heard someone say *"Come on, get a grip!"* to a person who's in fear or in anger mode?

Technology is advancing so quickly, it seems that those smart phones and tablets are not enough anymore. The world keeps demanding more and more at a faster and faster pace. Keeping track of everything that's taking place outside of us is becoming more and more difficult.

With all these outside distractions how can we expect to keep track of what is going on inside of us?

Just the sheer volume of e-mails we get daily is overwhelming. If I don't keep on clicking *unsubscribe* to marketing e-mail blasts, I will receive hundreds of e-mails every day, reaching me wherever I am, enticing me with fake and attainable discounts and purchase restrictions and fine prints just to entice me to buy junk I don't need. We also live in a world of instant gratification. With just one click on your smart phone, you can check out of your shopping cart in an instant. You even have that darn *"auto-ship"* option, no need to think anymore if you really need that product every month and at the same time. What if you don't want it the following month? But when you clicked the *"BUY"* button you were convinced it was what you wanted/needed every single month for the rest of your life and you couldn't live without it. And if a month later you changed your mind because *"now come to think of it"* you don't really want/ need it, you'll have to spend more time canceling, sometimes even paying fees and bla bla bla... What if you lose your phone? OMG...The planet would burst into flames, turn to ashes, and disintegrate into space. What a waste of time!!

Yes, I know what you're thinking. I'm exaggerating, and sometimes it's all very convenient. But my goodness, can we turn off the autopilot for a little while and look at where we are going? We are human *beings*, not human *doings*. Can we just stop doing and start being for a while? The state of being is just as important as the state of doing. *Doing* is physical, and *being* is nonphysical. Once again, being well balanced is the key.

As we have observed earlier, humans have a high tendency to develop habits. And those habits and patterns are reflected in our actions. If you observe the action, you'll find out what the pattern is. If it serves you well, keep it. If it doesn't serve you, change it or get rid of it altogether. That's easier said than done, I know, but you have to start somewhere. So start with the easier things, the things you know that need to go and can be changed quickly. Believe it or not, many times when I'm ready to make a new change, depending on what I'm working on, I start with my clothing. I never really liked shopping for clothes. I like variety as a general rule, but in some stores it can be overwhelming. So I would never go because I could not make a decision, and I would come back empty-handed with half of a day wasted. It would upset me every time. But I realized changing my outside look at first would help me with taking action/initiative and thus spark the momentum. So I donate the stuff I don't want anymore and head straight to the men's store. I ask the sales people for guidance on the trends, what would look good on me, and share what my "looking" goals are. No, I don't necessarily spend crazy amounts of money, and no, I don't go every week and certainly don't use this as "retail therapy". So you may say; *"You started on the outside looks first, dude!"* True it seems, but in reality, I started inside by changing the negative meaning, the negative label, of clothes shopping I had developed and transformed it into a new meaning, a new label, that empowered me and not paralyzed me. I like going clothes shopping now because I've made it fun and I've conditioned my mind that dressing well is a sign of success. It's something I want to do out of desire and not out of obligation. Can you see the difference? It's a great metaphor for change. We change clothes every day, and my new clothes remind me of my new goals. It is a simple and easy thing for me to do. Bite size changes, and build on each success. What would work for you? Look into it, and start making the changes.

So what can we do during these times of uncertainty, instability, and unpredictability? What can we rely on? Well, there's only one thing to do and that is to turn inward and start to learn the inner workings of the Soul/Heart/Body/Mind connection. You must become self-reliant. Once we start understanding our inner workings of our own inner world, we can then start to understand the outside world, the universe. Through meditation, self-reflection, and self-analysis, we can learn about ourselves and advance much quicker and much easier and achieve higher success in manifesting our desires and goals. Meditation helps you disconnect from the physical facets of life for a while and turn inward within the inner world of energy. Cleansing your energy field is like cleaning the windshield of your car. It allows you to see further, better, and broader. Cleansing your energy field is like cleaning your diamond. It allows more light to come in to become more brilliant and perhaps even become what is known as a *Beacon of Light,* often described as the Golden Bright Light. Twin Hearts Meditation offers that and much more. There are many levels of understanding and truth in everything. It all depends on our capacity to understand, to see, to experience and to accept what is truth. Those varying degrees of understanding come with inner experiences, a willingness to keep an open heart and mind and with proper guidance. The mine will reveal many beautiful and precious gems. The inner workings of the Soul/Heart/Body/ Mind are just the same. If you're willing to search on the surface or dig tirelessly within the depths of your Being, you will find the most magnificent diamonds waiting quietly for you to harvest them, cut them, and allow the light to come in and maximize their potential.

There are many levels and varying degrees of understanding. The Diamond analogy applies to virtually every aspect of life, society, economics, politics, science, human psychology, human physiology, and especially spirituality. There are also many principles that apply here, again with varying degrees of understanding. One of the keys and pillar is the Principle of Character Building. Without the constant application of this pillar, not much can or will be accomplished. Everything we do and everything we see is a direct reflection of what humans externalize from within, either individually or as a society. This is experienced on a personal level, family level, communities and countries all the way the planetary level as a whole. The effects of the filters and the angles of observation are tremendous. They can either help us move forward and evolve, or they can hold us back and sometimes even pressure us to regress. We must consciously decide to wake up, make wise choices, make decisions, and take action. And step by step, your path will be revealed to you.

We've only started to scratch the surface in the journey we've traveled in this book. There's so much more to it. I'd like to show you how deep the Diamond mine/mind goes and continue making more profound connections and parallels with human consciousness and higher spiritual development, but that's another story…